Sharon Norris Elliott

RAISING BOYS
To Be Like JESUS

Juliet,
Boys like Jesus
become men of God!

Love,
Sharon Elliott

JUDSON PRESS
PUBLISHERS SINCE 1824
VALLEY FORGE, PA

RAISING BOYS TO BE LIKE JESUS

© 2009 by Judson Press, Valley Forge, PA 19482-0851
All rights reserved.

Judson Press has made every effort to trace the ownership of all quotes. In the event of a question arising from the use of a quote, we regret any error made and will be pleased to make the necessary correction in future printings and editions of this book.

Unless otherwise indicated, all Scripture quotations are from the HOLY BIBLE, NEW INTERNATIONAL VERSION®. NIV®. Copyright © 1973, 1978, 1984 by International Bible Society. Used by permission of Zondervan. All rights reserved.

Scripture quotations marked KJV are from the King James Version of the Bible.

Library of Congress Cataloging-in-Publication Data
Elliott, Sharon Norris, 1957-
Raising boys to be like Jesus / Sharon Norris Elliott. — 1st ed.
p. cm.
ISBN 978-0-8170-1541-1 (pbk. : alk. paper) 1. Jesus Christ—Example. 2. Men (Christian theology) 3. Parenting—Religious aspects—Christianity. 4. Child rearing—Religious aspects—Christianity. I. Title.
BT304.2.E45 2009
248.8'45—dc22

2008045998

Printed in the U.S.A.
First Edition, 2009

To the men in my life:

MY DADDY, Vincent Isaiah Norris, who modeled what God was like every day of his life. Because of my daddy, I will recognize God when I see him.

MY HUSBAND, James D. Elliott, who lives as an example of godly manhood for our children.

OUR ELDEST SON, Jerod, who is continuing the legacy of excellent fatherhood with his son, Jerod Jr.

OUR YOUNGEST SONS, Matthew and Mark, the test cases for this book, who have proven that raising boys to be like Jesus can be done, because they reflect Christ's image.

I love you all.

CONTENTS

PREFACE

One day I looked one of my friends in the eye and said, "How come nobody told us all what we were signing up for when we decided to have kids?" I was being only 95 percent facetious. I meant every word of the other 5 percent.

Like you, I have had countless wonderful moments with my children, but I also have times in parenting when I am not exactly sure what to do and need help. And I have discovered that as my kids grow older, instead of the job getting simpler, it is getting more complicated. Explanations and decisions that used to be clear can sometimes be murky at best. "Because I said so" just doesn't always work as an answer anymore. I find myself using more and more intricate reasoning as my kids age.

I'm glad that early in my sons' lives, I asked myself, "How can I raise my boys to be godly individuals?" My logic was simple. If God could trust them, then I could trust them. If they were intent on pleasing God, then I would automatically be pleased with them as well. I didn't know how complicated things would get as my boys got older, so I started following a plan. All my parenting decisions would be centered on the example and teachings of the Lord. I chose to face any decision, challenge, or perplexity concerning my children by asking, "What can I do at this point in time that will help my boys become more like Christ?" What better example to point them to than Jesus Christ—the one whose total life involved pleasing God?

Thus the focus of this book is raising boys to be like Jesus. A generation of sons whose lives are patterned after the Master's will profoundly impact society. In a world used to failure due to dysfunctional families, cheating CEOs, and immoral politicians, our Christlike sons will succeed as loving husbands, honest businessmen, and stable citizens. Let's launch out on this journey to reform our parenting techniques. Let's follow Jesus as he passes through the various stages of his life, gleaning as we go principles that will help us raise our sons in his image.

HOW TO USE THIS BOOK

We buy books for lots of reasons—information, education, obligation, exasperation, and entertainment. If you are an expectant parent, you are probably reading this book for information. The day-to-day realities of parenting have not yet hit, so you have the time to leisurely take in this information and store it for later use. This book can be used as a lesson plan of sorts as you apply these principles from day one after your son's birth.

As a new parent or as the parent of a toddler, you're reading this book for the purpose of education. You are off the bench and on the field of play, and no matter what child-rearing advice you received before you actually held your son, you are feeling as if you still need assistance. This book will function for you in the same way that regular vaccinations function for your child—to ward off problems before they can take hold.

You have already discovered the Bible is correct in its assessment that every human being is born with a sin nature. This volume will supply you with practical tips for directing your son's spiritual growth. I suggest you make it your overriding goal to parallel your son's development with Christ's. Since the chapters of this book are arranged in the chronological order of events in Jesus' life, you can start while your son is a baby and lay the foundation discussed in chapter 1. As he grows through the toddler years, make spiritual things a part of his life as described in chapter 2 and start teaching about discernment and consequences as outlined in chapter 3. While your son continues to mature slowly but steadily, continue to pour the lessons of the successive chapters into his life and spirit.

Those of you with sons in elementary and middle school may be picking up this book out of a sense of obligation. You are at the parenting stage in which you are obligated to keep things running smoothly in your son's life. It's like taking your son to the doctor for regular checkups and relatively small injuries. You do this to be sure everything remains okay. This book will assist you with that keep-life-running-smoothly obligation. Use the chapters as regular checkups.

Perhaps you never heard of the benefits of some of the techniques suggested here, or maybe you have just made a commitment to Christ yourself and now want to communicate this wonderful new life to your pre-adolescent son. As you read, you may find that you have missed some "vaccinations" and your son is showing symptoms of having picked up ideas that run counter to what you now want him to understand. This book will supply you with easy-to-implement activities that will make it possible to infuse Christlike qualities into your son's life. Read and begin implementing the foundational points of chapters 1 and 2; then feel free to read the other chapters in the order of the issues that present themselves in your home. Try not to leave any chapters unread, as there are nuggets of valuable guidance in each one.

If you have bought or received this book and your son is already in high school, your reason for reading it may be exasperation. I can pretty much guarantee that is how you feel if you have never heard of or tried to implement these ideas. You will use this book as a resource manual, applying the principles in order of the crises that arise. For you, it's time for intensive care. Every moment of influence counts, for you have only one to four years to have a daily impact. Be of good cheer—it can be done. Be deliberate yet not overbearing; be loving and determined. The internalization of most of these principles now will happen as more a function of conversation with your son and modeling before your son than of personal implementation for him.

My desire for all readers is that this book also supplies a level of entertainment. For this cause, you will find anecdotes sprinkled throughout each chapter that will hopefully humanize each principle and help to make this journey enjoyable. Every chapter also contains "Step Aside" segments to assist you in personalizing each principle to operate most effectively in your home and in your son's development.

The first words of Proverbs 22:6 (KJV) are directed to parents emphatically: "Train up a child. . . ." The training of your son is your primary responsibility and duty. What better tracking device of your progress as a successful parent can there be but to watch your son's development as he stands inch for inch, measuring up to the growth chart that mirrors the life of Christ?

1
The Infant Son Lying in the Manger
Laying a Spiritual Foundation

Matthew 1:18-25; Luke 1:26-45; 2:1-24, 39

"It's a boy."

Those words began my odyssey in actual practice as a mother. I was the mother of a son. I understand that I was my child's mother from the moment he was conceived, but something altogether different happened when I held him—my son—against my chest, looked down into his tiny face, and found him gazing back as if to say, "I'm here; now what are you going to do?"

Actually, I started out pretty confidently. I hadn't gone to the prenatal classes because I had to be off my feet those last two months due to a sudden hernia flair-up that required a minor operation. Still, I watched videos about the birthing process and read lots of books about what to expect once the baby was born. I was ready, and if Matthew had been able to ask me that question, I probably would have answered, "Kid, I am 'Mother.' Don't you worry about a thing. I've got this!"

Of course, that was before I got out of the hospital and away from the help of the nurses.

Once Matthew was home, he could not settle down. He cried pretty much nonstop. Nothing worked. I fed him; he cried. I burped him; he cried. I changed him; he cried. I bathed him; he cried. I'd listened intently to *Focus on the Family* and was convinced that first day that I had one of those strong-willed children. We were sitting in the pediatrician's office the very next morning.

Well, as it turned out, nothing was wrong with my baby. He was just getting used to his new surroundings and my handling of him. As the days went on, we fell into a routine and things calmed down. Now it was time for me to pull information from my prenatal self-education and concentrate on what I needed to do to raise my son as he should be raised.

What did I want to do for Matthew? Well, I wanted to raise him to be smart, but not just smart, wise. I wanted to show him how to be happy, but not just happy, contented. I wanted to instruct him on how to be a friend, but more than a friend, a loyal and true person. My list went on and on. Most of all, I wanted to raise him to be a man of God who would grow to know, love, and live for God. Those same desires became doubly important twenty-one months later when I gave birth to another son, Mark.

Because you are reading this book, I assume you probably hold some of the same kinds of desires for your son as I held for mine. I daresay Mary, Jesus' mother, likely had those same desires too. Although she knew her Son was God's Son, she was a human woman becoming a mother for the first time.

Step Aside

List some of the desires you have for your son:

_____

_____

_____

_____

_____

_____

_____

_____

_____

Therefore, aspects of her story give us insights into the first components necessary to raise our sons in her Son's image.

The Facts

The story of Jesus' birth may be one of the most well-known Bible stories in our culture. Christians and nonbelievers alike know at least some aspects of it because of the popularity of the Christmas holiday, which, despite the efforts of political correctness, can't be separated from its origin.

This amazing but true story records that a young virgin girl by the name of Mary was engaged to a man named Joseph when she heard from the angel Gabriel that she was pregnant. Needless to say, she was quite surprised and at first extremely troubled at what Gabriel was saying to her. Nevertheless, the angel allayed her fears by assuring her that this pregnancy was of God. God delighted in her and was honoring her by choosing her to birth his own Son into the world. Gabriel followed up this assurance with proof that God could do anything by telling Mary that her elderly cousin, Elizabeth, was six months pregnant even as they spoke. This convinced Mary that nothing was impossible with God, and she submitted to God's plan.

We don't know how much time elapsed between the angel's visit and Mary's revelation of the news to Joseph, so she may or may not have been excited to tell him this strange story. If she told him right away, she was probably wide-eyed, breathless, and talking really fast. If she waited awhile, fear could have begun to settle in as she had time to reflect on how her society scorned unwed mothers. Whether she told him right away or waited, we know his reaction was one of disbelief. He immediately formulated a plan to divorce her quietly and put her away somewhere so as not to expose her to public humiliation.

Joseph soon rethought his plan after a heavenly visit of his own. The angel of the Lord convinced Joseph that Mary was telling the truth and that it would be his job to take Mary as his wife and be this baby's stepfather. After being told what to name the baby and what the baby's name meant, Joseph obeyed the command of God and took Mary home as his spouse.

Mary returned home, and the next information Scripture gives us is that a census would be taken that required the movement of masses of people. Everyone was required to return to the town of his birth to register, so Joseph had to take his family to Bethlehem because he was a descendant of David. The timing couldn't have seemed worse, because Mary was at the end of her ninth month, "ready to pop." And that she did, in a stable, because all the inns were booked with people in town for the census. Still, all was done according to prophecy, down to the last detail, and the new parents were very careful to follow the Mosaic law, making Jesus' first outing a trip to the temple on his eighth day of life to be circumcised.

The Son of God had come into the world, and we can glean principles from the very beginning of his life that can help us encourage our sons to reflect his image throughout their lives.

The Right Soil

It is no secret that to build anything sturdy, the structure must be established on a solid, even ground. Consider the Tower of Pisa. Although it is famous now and no one would dare think of straightening it, the tower should not be leaning. It is sinking into the soft river valley sediments on which it rests. The sandy, marshy, unstable soil is the reason for the tower's lean.[1]

It is a good idea to choose the right soil on which to build the lives of our sons even before they are born so they will be sturdy, godly men. Now don't panic. You may be reading this book as a parent of a son who is already five, ten, or fifteen years old. That's fine. You can still benefit from this discussion on soil selection. You have heard of repotting plants, haven't you? You repot a plant because it needs a fresh start. You parents with sons already born can think of this section as repotting mix for your son, while expectant parents can start preparing the "soil."

Whether your son is already here or not, the result will be the same. You will have sons who won't grow with a permanent lean; they will grow straight, reflecting a clear, steady image of Christ. Three elements compose the right soil—the mother, the father, and family planning.

The Mother Moms, look at the selection of Mary, the mother of Jesus. God's message to her was this: "Hail, thou that art highly favoured, the Lord is with thee: blessed art thou among women" (Luke 1:28 KJV).

Wow! Now that's a greeting. Let's break this down. First, Gabriel says Mary is "highly favoured." This means she has been endued with special honor, made acceptable in some unique way. Second, he says she is "blessed . . . among women." "Blessed" here means "to speak well of" or "to praise." God speaks to Mary through Gabriel, saying that she has received his grace and is being given a special honor. In relation to all other women, she is praiseworthy. This is the kind of woman God chose to be the mother of his Son.

Ladies, let me put this to you straight. Are you living the praise-worthy life of one chosen by God for the task of raising a son? In essence God is saying to you, "Here, I want you to be the mother of my son," for as the psalmist says, "Sons are a heritage from the LORD, children a reward from him" (Psalm 127:3).

One of the first steps in preparing the right soil in which to raise your son is to take a good look at your own life. I did some serious self-evaluation when I was pregnant with Matthew. The main thought that ran through my mind was, *What will my children say about their mother when they grow up?* Knowing that children will tell the truth about their parents sooner or later, it mattered to me what that truth would be, so I made some decisions then and there about how I would live from then on. My life was no longer about me, myself, and I. I wanted my life and lifestyle to have a positive effect on my children. I didn't want to be an embarrassment to them, an impediment to their future, or a hindrance to their ability to love God. I thought about such things as the way I would dress. How would I present myself when I attended parent-teacher meetings, for example? I wasn't one to curse, but I put it in my mind anyway that I did not want my children hearing nasty words coming from my mouth. How would I want them to see me react to criticism and disappointment? What would they learn from me about handling money? I considered lots of different things. I'll admit, I haven't always met my own standard, but I have given it a valiant effort and am pretty pleased so far with what I have heard my boys—now young adults—say to others about me.

Step Aside
List some of the lifestyle changes you want to make to be a better example of godliness to your son.

_____

_____

_____

_____

_____

_____

_____

_____

_____

_____

The Father We live in a disposable, fast, alterable, unstable world, and our family structure is caught up in the ever-fluctuating tide. Christian marriages end at the same rate as non-Christian ones do. Our churches are finding themselves ministering to an ever-growing population of single-parent families, these families usually being led by single mothers. According to the U.S. Census Bureau, 59 percent of all American kids will live in a single-parent home at least once in their lifetime, and currently 16 million children live in single-parent homes.[2] Many of these mothers are doing an amazing job—I was one of this number for a while. Most of those mothers will also acknowledge how difficult it is to raise a child alone. Biologically speaking, it takes two to conceive, and therefore it isn't surprising that after the labor of childbirth is over and the hard work of raising the child begins, the ideal parenting model features two active adults in the home—a mother and a father. We must, then, take into consideration the significance of a godly man's influence in the lives of our sons. A man's type of care is a vital element of the good soil we need on which to start building the strong character we want our sons to exhibit.

Joseph was Jesus' earthly father. It took a little convincing—okay, it took a lot of convincing, an angelic visit to be precise—but Joseph entered into God's plan with Mary, stepped up to the plate, and did what he had to do. He married Mary and cared for her during this first pregnancy.

The most important thing a father can do for his son is to love that child's mother. Everyone in the home feels the balance provided by this love. When Father loves Mother, Father will be concerned about her emotional, physical, and psychological well-being. That sense of well-being spills directly over into the well-being of the children. So Father's love of Mother is also evident in his care for their children. Sons learn how to treat women by watching their father's tenderness toward their mother and by watching how he participates in the management of household responsibilities. This picture will be a reference point for them when they are grown and take on families of their own.

My friend Chara found herself in a marriage that had turned sour. Her husband, Nate, had decided he could no longer handle the responsibilities of their life together. Their relationship, the children, the mortgage, the bills—all were too much for him to manage, and he gave up. Chara was no longer being loved as their wedding vows had declared she should be. On top of that, Nate became physically violent at home and frequented gentleman's clubs.

Chara had never expected even the possibility of this situation in which she found herself. Not only were her emotional, psychological, and physical needs not being met, but they were being trampled on. The couple's sons began to show signs of the strain through poor school grades, jumpiness, and misbehavior. When things worsened in the home even after several years of prayer and counseling, Chara made the difficult decision to separate from Nate. Her decision was driven largely by her concern for the effect of the tension on her sons. She was determined to keep her sons from internalizing from their father's behavior that said it was okay to shirk their responsibilities as husbands, okay to terrorize their families, and okay to disrespect women and be violent toward them.

Almost as soon as Chara and the boys moved, she began to see positive change in her sons. They were settled, and their grades improved, as did their behavior. Sometime after the divorce, Chara met and married Trent, a wonderful godly man who demonstrates his love for her by treating her with tenderness, handling his family responsibilities, and talking things out rationally. The boys see how much Trent cares for their mom, and they have quickly come to love and respect him too. Trent has drawn them into his life as his own sons, and they have taken to him as more than a stepdad. He is the correct example of father care Chara's sons have needed.

But Chara is fortunate; not all women in a similar situation find a man like Trent. Maybe you are a woman who doesn't have a man in your life who is fathering your sons. What are you supposed to do in light of the need to start your sons out on good soil? Remember, technically, Jesus was an "unplanned pregnancy," a surprise yet not a mistake. Mary was not legally married when she became pregnant, but God knew how and when his Son would come into the world just as he was aware of everything about your son long before you were. He is never surprised by an unintentional pregnancy or by a death or divorce that leaves sons without a father. Just keep in mind that no child is illegitimate.

Single-parent mothers of sons need Josephs. In the same way Joseph stepped in for Mary's son, there are Josephs who will step in for the sons of single moms. During the three years of my separation and divorce when I was living as a single mom, several Josephs operated in the lives of my boys and me. We had positive Christian role models in our pastors, the boys' uncles, grown male cousins, and other trustworthy men in the church. Even my girlfriends' husbands would tease my boys, wrestle with them, and take them on outings so they could do some male bonding. I remember how I appreciated my ex-husband's father hanging out with Mark, my youngest son, as they enjoyed watching NBA games together. We have all heard that it takes a village to raise a child, and that's true. It can't hurt to surround your sons with Josephs, even if there is a loving Christian male role model in the home.

Notice that I said my boys were around trustworthy men. New "uncles" unleash all sorts of confusing emotions, set up false hopes, and add new relationships to your sons' lives that might not be permanent. If you are a single mother, no matter how lonely you are, it is not a good idea to bring a new boyfriend into your sons' lives until you are fairly sure the relationship may lead to marriage.

Step Aside

1. If you are separated or divorced, how are you handling that situation? How does Scripture guide your decisions and responses? How are you communicating with your sons about their new family situation?

2. If your sons have a father who is active in their lives and a great Christian role model, take time to thank God now for that wonderful man.

3. If your sons do not have their father, pray for God to send "Josephs" into their lives, men qualified by their godly lifestyles to mentor your sons and supply them with life lessons on being men of which God can be proud. Never forget that Jesus is the ultimate role model for you son. Continue to point your son toward becoming like Christ.

I am now married to a wonderful "Joseph." His name is James, and at our wedding, after we exchanged our vows, he made a vow to my boys, making them "our" boys. He is living up to those vows by loving their mother and being a fabulous example of Christian manhood in our home. His presence in their lives is supplying them with the good soil that only a father can provide.

Through nature and nurture, children do indeed take on the characteristics of their parents, and if we have made unwise choices concerning our parenting partner, we may face some negative consequences for those choices. Those consequences might be learned behaviors or personality traits in our children that cause us to lose our tempers or our sleep or worse. If so, we have our work cut out for us.

Thankfully, spiritual truths outweigh earthly realities. First Corinthians 2:12-14 says:

> We have not received the spirit of the world but the Spirit who is from God, that we may understand what God has freely given us. This is what we speak, not in words taught us by human wisdom but in words taught by the Spirit, expressing spiritual truths in spiritual words. The man without the Spirit does not accept the things that come from the Spirit of God, for they are foolishness to him, and he cannot understand them, because they are spiritually discerned.

Step Aside

List negative qualities you have observed in your son. Beside each negative quality, find a counteractive Bible verse you can apply to the retraining of your son in that area. For example:

Negative quality: violent temper
Counteractive Bible verse: Better a patient man than a warrior, a man who controls his temper than one who takes a city (Proverbs 16:32).

God gives us wisdom to know what qualities we should implant in our sons. Godly qualities can choke out even naturally inbred carnal tendencies as we direct our sons' growth. We will see our sons mature as Mary's Son did: "in wisdom and stature, and in favor with God and men" (Luke 2:52).

Family Planning The third element of the right soil in which to start to grow spiritually strong sons is family planning. At first glance, you may think I'm talking about birth control. I'm not.

The family planning I'm referring to here is having a plan for your son's spiritual direction. You will have this third necessary element if you put a plan in place for how you will direct your son spiritually. Many of us know that we should eat five servings of fruits and vegetables per day and exercise regularly. We know how much good it will do us, yet we don't ever get around to it. That is because we don't have a serious plan in place to implement the diet and exercise changes. In the same way, we know there are some things we ought to do to head our sons in the right spiritual direction, but we simply haven't taken the time to draw up a serious plan to help us get around to implementation.

Joseph followed God's plan in putting his family together and taking them to where they needed to be. He took Mary to be his wife to set up the necessary family structure. Then he took them to Bethlehem so that the Messiah would be born in the exact town where prophecy had predicted he would be. Of course he probably didn't know that is what he was doing when he followed the dictates of the census, but the point is that he obeyed God and everything turned out as it should have.

Mary and Joseph's plan was to follow God's plan in relation to raising their Son. If we want our sons to grow up in the image of Christ, we too need to determine to follow God's plan for them. For the rest of this chapter, we will look at what Mary and Joseph did to lay a spiritual foundation for their Son who grew up to be the Messiah. If we lay the same foundation, surely our sons can grow up in his image.

A Firm Foundation

Now that we have chosen the right soil containing the elements of the mother, the father, and a family plan, let's build on the soil a firm foundation. The elements or planks of that foundation will be the stuff of the rest of this book; however the overarching starting point to this whole process is to have one thought in mind: after all is said and done, you want your son to become like Christ.

Obviously, Joseph and Mary cannot be an example to us concerning introducing our sons to their Son. That is our responsibility. Our sons will not desire to grow up to be like Christ unless he is perceived in their minds as someone worthy of emulation.

In our home we make Jesus Christ as familiar to our sons as other close family members. Jesus' presence in our lives is as real and as essential as our need for sleep and food. Be sure though, that there are specific times when you pointedly ask your son if he has a personal relationship with Christ. God has no grandchildren. Your son is not a Christian just because you are.

The following passages are addressed to every individual regardless of the spiritual background of his or her parents:

■ For all have sinned and fall short of the glory of God (Romans 3:23).
■ God demonstrates his own love for us in this: While we were still sinners, Christ died for us (Romans 5:8).
■ The wages of sin is death, but the gift of God is eternal life in Christ Jesus our Lord (Romans 6:23).
■ If you confess with your mouth, "Jesus is Lord," and believe in your heart that God raised him from the dead, you will be saved. For it is with your heart that you believe and are justified, and it is with your mouth that you confess and are saved (Romans 10:9-10).

When I invite dinner guests to my home, I do all the work. I clean my home, shop for the food, and cook the meal. I set the table with linen napkins in gold napkin rings, rose-patterned china, ornate tableware, and fine crystal. All my guests have to do is show up and avail themselves of all that has been freely provided for them. In the same way, God has freely provided the way of salvation for your son. But like any invited guest, your son has to take the initiative and accept the invitation.

I was driving to Bible study one night with five-year-old Matthew seat-belted into his booster seat when he said he wanted to be a Christian. As I maneuvered through traffic, I helped Matthew to pray and confess his belief in Jesus as his Lord and Savior. Mark experienced becoming a Christian more gradually through home exposure to Christ, Sunday school, and Christian school lessons. He made a confession of his faith and belief on his own. When I asked him one day if he was a Christian, he was offended. "Of course I am," he responded. "How could you ask a question like that?" I told him it was my job as his mom to be sure he'd be in heaven one day. Both boys knew their baptisms were the outward sign of the miraculous work Christ had done on the inside.

Be sure to give your son opportunities to ask the same question the keeper of the prison asked Paul and Silas in Acts 16:30: "What must I do to be saved?" Then be ready to respond. The importance of the need for salvation, as well as all the other things that will be mentioned in this book, must be tackled consistently and deliberately. All of this is much too important to leave to chance.

NOTES

1. Albert G. Ingalls, "The 'Sinking' Tower of Pisa," *Scientific American*, February 1929, http://www.endex.com/gf/buildings/hpisa/hpinfo/SciAm0229; Joan Steen, "The Leaning Tower Is Falling Down," *Popular Science*, September 1960, http://www.pisabelltower.com/tparticles/popsci961.

2. Children's Living Arrangements and Characteristics: March 2002. Demographic Programs, Current Population Reports. By Jason Fields. Issued June 2003. http://www.census.gov/prod/2003pubs/p20-547.pdf.

2
The Adolescent Debating in the Temple

Luke 2:41-52

One of the most devastating feelings I ever experienced as a mom was the desperate anxiety of not knowing where my child was. I had put the boys to bed about an hour earlier and was performing the routine bed check before I retired to my room for the night. Fully expecting to see their precious faces peacefully resting on their pillows, imagine my alarm when I discovered Matthew was not in his top bunk. At seven years old, he had decided he didn't really want a room to himself and had recently moved himself back in to double up with his little brother.

Maybe he changed his mind, I thought as I headed toward the other bedroom. The idea calmed me as I tiptoed into the other room and peeked my head around the corner. Another empty bed. Now my heart began to race a little. No more tipping around, I hurried to the living room. Both sofas held only the cushions and pillows. As I rounded the corner to the den, I figured, *He must have tried to watch more TV and fell asleep on the couch in there.* No such luck. There was only one more logical place to look, and that was my bed, in which my kids never slept.

After not finding Matthew there, I was really concerned. I retraced my steps and rechecked all the rooms. The doors and windows were closed and locked, so I was certain no intruder had carried him away, but where could he be? The only places I hadn't checked were the bathrooms. Lo and behold, there he was, sound asleep in the bathtub, huddled up with his favorite blanket. He did not even awaken as I carried him back to his bed.

I will never know what prompted that child to sleep in the tub, but the incident helped me to identify, however slightly, with Mary and Joseph's panic when, on their way back from the Passover, they realized they didn't know where the then twelve-year-old Jesus was. This incident seems to have been the first time they were separated from their first and very special son. As they frantically searched, they must have thought, *Where is he? What is he doing? Who is he with? Is he all right?*

We won't always be around our sons either. Where will they go? What will they do? Who will they be with? Will they be all right? These are all important questions. Can we ever be comfortable thinking about our sons' well-being when we are not around? Will they use common sense? What can we do as parents to help assure that the truth we have taught our sons will be the truth that has been caught and internalized by them? Let's see what Jesus did when he got away from his parents.

Jesus Held to His Established Habit of Service to God

We learn in Luke 2:41-42 that "every year [Jesus'] parents went to Jerusalem for the Feast of the Passover. When he was twelve years old, they went up to the Feast, according to the custom."

By the time Jesus was twelve, he was in the habit of participating in spiritual service. His parents, Joseph and Mary, established this habit in their son early. They took him as an infant to Jerusalem to present him to the Lord (see Luke 2:22). They further obeyed the Old Testament law and took him back to the temple to have him circumcised when he was eight days old. We are not surprised, then, that it was the habit of this family to travel the forty-five-mile trek from Nazareth to Jerusalem to celebrate the Passover, their religion's holiest feast held in their religion's holiest place.

I remember my daddy taking our family on annual, cross-country road trips, but we traveled those miles on paved, interstate highways in air-conditioned Chryslers. No such luxury for Jesus' family. Those forty-five miles were probably covered on foot or donkey. Nevertheless, like Jesus' family trip, ours always included a week's stop at a spiritual event, our denomination's annual convention. And we not only attended, we participated. My father was instrumental in organizing the event, my mother was involved in the women's activities, and when I was old enough, I took a leadership role in the annual youth section. The habit of service established early in my life is now my personal commitment, which keeps me heavily involved, not only in my local church, but in Christian service as my vocation.

When Jesus grew up, he too continued this habit of faithful service to the local assembly. We see it not only in our current text, but carried on in his ministry. Whenever he traveled to a new city, he and the disciples entered the local synagogue to teach (see Mark 1:21, 38-39; Luke 4:43). I believe this habit to attend synagogue regularly was established in Jesus early by his parents' diligence in consistently taking him as he was growing up.

This point of application is easy: if you want your son to be

Step Aside

1. Do you attend church regularly? If not, why not? When do you intend to start?

2. If you are looking for a church to attend, do you know people who attend church? What do they have to say about their church? If they use phrases like, "Our pastor's sermons help us grow in the Lord," and "Our church helps us understand the Word," then it is a good idea to ask them if you can visit with them. These phrases mean that the focus of the church is on God and the Bible, and that's what you want. Your friends should be glad to take you along.

a regular churchgoer, establish the habit by taking him to church regularly. Notice, I didn't say *send* him; I said *take* him. As Hebrews 10:25 says, "Let us not give up meeting together, as some are in the habit of doing."

Because Sunday school, Sunday morning worship service, and other church activities have been a regular part of my sons' lives since birth, they have no story to tell about when they were not in church. Jesus seems to have had that same testimony, because at twelve years old, when his parents wondered where he was, they found him in a familiar place—the temple—having a discussion with the religious leaders. Jesus grew up being comfortable in God's place and with God's people. Our sons will grow up the same way if we keep them connected with the church.

As parents, we are responsible for the spiritual upbringing of our sons, so it is vitally important that we choose a church home that will be an accurate reflection and extension of what we are trying to impart. The common cultural saying, "It takes a village to raise a child," applies in this context as well. Within the loving confines of our worship community, our sons can be fully nourished—mind, body, and soul. My sons' lasting friendships have been forged in the church. The men outside our home to whom they turn for mentoring are men from the church. The women, apart from their family members, who provide good examples of godly femininity, are in the church.

Jesus Looked for Answers in the Church

After the Feast was over, while his parents were returning home, the boy Jesus stayed behind in Jerusalem, but they were unaware of it. Thinking he was in their company, they traveled on for a day. Then they began looking for him among their relatives and friends. When they did not find him, they went back to Jerusalem to look for him. After three days they found him in the temple courts, sitting

17

among the teachers, listening to them and asking them questions. (Luke 2:43-46)

What a place for Jesus to be found: in the temple courts, sitting among the teachers. And what a thing to find him doing: listening to those teachers and asking them questions. We are not told exactly what Jesus was asking, but to be sure, Joseph and Mary could trust the answers he was receiving because they knew and trusted the people to whom Jesus was exposed.

Once you have chosen a church where the Word of God is taught accurately and the practical application of the Word is encouraged vigorously, be sure the assembly has an active youth group and responsible youth leaders who are espousing the Christian virtues and values taught in Scripture. Make it a requirement that your son participate in the youth activities. Those responsible youth leaders are very important, because especially during the teen years, they can be the ones who will come alongside you and reinforce the values your son may begin to question.

After being involved for years in college-bound programs and college prep classes, seventeen-year-old Camron decided on Hampton University as his first choice college to attend. Then suddenly he started discussing with his mom about how college isn't for everybody. Shocked, his mom, Teri, questioned him about the source of this new mind-set.

It turns out that Camron had been talking to some friends at school—friends who had no plans after high school. These buddies, who probably weren't prepared for college, had decided that college wasn't really necessary after all. They could join the military or get jobs, and they would be okay. Teri could see all Camron's years of hard work evaporating into either camouflage or a dead-end nine-to-five. She quickly nipped those ideas in the bud by pointing out to Camron that, while there is nothing wrong with serving one's country and there is certainly nothing wrong with a strong work ethic, a university education would give him a lot of other options. Camron was also involved in a Rites of Passage program at his church led by his own father and other men whose advice reinforced Teri's messages. By the end of the conversation, Camron was back on the road to graduating high school with honors and packing his trunk for Hampton.

Thankfully, Camron and Teri had a track record of being able to talk about things calmly and rationally. Camron knew he could trust his mother's opinion and evaluation of his ideas. However, even if our sons don't talk to us about everything, if we put them in a church around people they can trust and to whom they will open up, we can rest assured that messages they do receive will be along the same lines as what we espouse as important.

Jesus Amazed People by His Answers

Luke 2:47-49 tells us that "everyone who heard [Jesus] was amazed at his understanding and his answers. When his parents saw him, they were astonished. His mother said to him, 'Son, why have you treated us like this? Your father and I have been anxiously searching for you.' 'Why were you searching for me?' he asked. 'Didn't you know I had to be in my Father's house?'"

In other words, Jesus was in the temple busy discussing issues that were important to his heavenly Father. In order for our sons to be like Jesus, they too need to be able to discuss issues important to God the Father. In an age that pushes the idea that right and wrong are relative, it is more important than ever to be sure our sons hold a biblical worldview, a mind-set that thinks as God thinks about the issues of life. Absolute truth exists. There are rights and there are wrongs. If your son were asked his opinion about life issues, what would he say? What does he know about his faith and God's expectations? Does he own his faith, and does he have a biblical worldview?

Encourage your son to think spiritually. You want your son's viewpoint on the issues of life to be the same as God's viewpoint on those issues. Romans 12:2 says, "Do not conform any longer to the pattern of this world, but be transformed by the renewing of your mind. Then you will be able to test and approve what God's will is—his good, pleasing and perfect will."

You do realize that your son is forming his own opinions about everything. He has an opinion about masculinity, femininity, motherhood, fatherhood, family, friendship, and respect for authority. He has viewpoints about sexuality, lying, cheating, stealing, homosexuality, and the church. He has something to say about how money should be spent, how the government makes decisions, and how his school should be run. As your son matures, he is internalizing all he sees and hears, and is processing it into the moral code by which he will live his adult life.

Do you know what your son's viewpoints are? How can you find out? Keep the lines of communication open and determine to listen when your son talks. Then allow the Holy Spirit to guide your understanding and your tongue. He will direct your understanding so you can discern the underlying spiritual issues on which your son's comments rest. He will also give you the words to say as you reason together, seeking the mind of God on the point in question.

When our oldest son Matthew turned fourteen, he asked to go see his first horror movie. We had had many discussions throughout the years about guarding our minds and hearts, because once something enters, the viewer can never erase the image. He said he remembered and understood those concepts, but was now mature enough to handle the fact that it was only a movie. I prayed and allowed him to go. A few days after the movie, I asked Matthew to tell me about the movie and what he thought of it. In a very nonchalant tone, he began to relate the events of the film. Following his initial general comments, he started telling me how he felt about the main character who was a boy about his own age.

"The boy's mother died, and he had to live with people he did not even know." Matthew's brow wrinkled as he empathized with this kid. "But then he learned some magic and brought his mom back to life."

Step Aside

You may be surprised at what your child has heard and understands. Further, you may also be surprised at what your child has heard and misunderstands. Take an inventory of your own opinions, viewpoints, and perspectives. Consider the following issues. Be honest and ask yourself the following evaluation questions regarding the items in the list:

What is my current viewpoint on this issue?

What is God's viewpoint on this issue?

How must I adjust my thinking to line up with how God views this issue?

abortion	education	motherhood
adultery	family	premarital sex
authority	fatherhood	racial issues
cheating	forgiveness	saving money
church	friendship	stealing
citizenship	homosexuality	substance use and abuse
commitment	lying	tithing
death		

Now ask your son his opinions and viewpoints about the items in the list.

Are his viewpoints the same as yours?

Are they consistent with what you understand the Bible says about each issue?

If either your views or your son's views differ from biblical truth, what do you plan to do to change those views so they line up with what God has said?

As other issues come to mind, add them to the list and go through the evaluation questions. Look for God to give you opportunities to share with your son what you are learning about how God wants you to think.

My spiritual antennae went up, because the Bible teaches that necromancy—attempted communication with the dead—is a sin (Deuteronomy 18:10-13).

Matthew continued, "That's what I would want to do if anything ever happened to you."

As sweet as that was, Matthew's thinking was veering away from scriptural truth. I had thought nightmares would have been his problem, but the result was much worse. From this one movie, he had begun to feel favorable toward a viewpoint that God expressly forbids. While there is nothing wrong with loving his mother and not wanting her to die, there is everything wrong with thinking that it is okay and even cool to conjure her back from the dead. This was a clear case of wrong thinking spiritually. After our discussion Matthew was able to see the error in his thinking in the light of God's Word.

To guide your son into correct spiritual thinking, you have to know the Word well yourself. As Christians, it is our responsibility to have an intimate relationship with God. As our thoughts begin to align with God's, our actions will reflect our godly viewpoints, and our sons will catch the godly perspective on life that we are passing on to them.

Jesus Continued to Obey His Parents and Grow in All Areas of Life

In Luke 2:50-51 we read that when Mary and Joseph heard Jesus' explanation for why he had stayed behind at the temple, "they did not understand what he was saying to them. Then he went down to Nazareth with them and was obedient to them."

Since we know that Jesus Christ is God in the flesh, it sounds a little strange to discuss how he obeyed his earthly parents, but that is exactly what he did. As parents of sons who are becoming like Jesus, we cannot be afraid of insisting on their obedience. You are your son's parent, not one of his buddies. Don't be scared to discipline him.

Throughout my career of teaching high school students, I have never ceased to be amazed at how some of the parents of the students I have taught over the years have been afraid to discipline their boys. During a parent-teacher conference once, I sat with the parents of a fifteen-year-old boy who was failing all of his classes. The parents were at the end of their rope with this young man and asked my suggestions as to what they should do to help turn him around. Since he obviously wasn't doing homework in the evenings, I inquired about his after-school activities. The parents responded that he just went into his room and closed the door.

I then turned to the young man and asked, "What do you do in your room after school?"

To my amazement, even with his parents sitting there, he refused to answer me, and the parents did not insist he reply. I then called him by name, and in a decidedly more forceful tone, I asked the question again.

"I'm talking to you, Evan," I repeated. "Look at me."

He looked up and met my gaze.

"Now answer my question. What do you do in your room when you get home from school?"

I refused to move my gaze from his, and finally he recognized my authority, but through a sneer he answered, "I play my video games and watch TV until she says dinner is ready."

I then looked back at his parents, surprised again at the fact that his mother exhibited no reaction to being called "she," and his father allowed his son to be so disrespectful to two women. This boy's parents basically shrugged their shoulders and gave me a look that said, "See, we told you we couldn't do anything with him."

Mind you, this child had several hundred dollars of technology on his hip. He carried to school a Bluetooth-enabled cell phone and a separate text-messaging device. When I suggested that they remove the video game system and television from his room and confiscate his communication devices, he silently bristled and they visibly recoiled.

"Why should Evan enjoy all these luxuries when he refuses to take care of his responsibilities?" I asked.

Their answer stunned me and basically ended our meeting, "If we take those things, he'll be mad at us."

What more was there to discuss? I certainly couldn't get Evan to complete college preparatory school work that required thought, discipline, and suspension of his fun in order to be prepared for a future as a responsible adult if his parents allowed him to enjoy privileges for merely existing. Our school refused to give him passing grades for no work, so instead of insisting on their son's compliance, his parents decided to withdraw him and enroll him in another school.

Even though Mary and Joseph were raising the Son of God, they insisted on Jesus' obedience and he submitted to them. They were the adults, and they took their role seriously. We must do the same. Insist on obedience from your son; then follow through with appropriate punishments that fit the infractions.

Annette's son, Philip, brought home a report card with several Ds. The low grades were a reflection of the fact that Philip was goofing off. Annette took her other children off of trash detail and assigned that chore to Philip until the next report card. Her rationale was simple: with grades like these, probably the best career Philip would get would be as a trash collector, and she wanted him to be properly prepared for the job. After six weeks of trash duty, Philip's next report card reflected significantly better grades.

Another part of discipline involves allowing the consequences of your son's actions to take their toll. I will discuss this at length in chapter 4.

Jesus Grew (Matured) in All Areas of Life

The final section of the passage we are considering in this chapter says, "And Jesus grew in wisdom and stature, and in favor with God and men" (Luke 2:52). Parents, you are responsible for providing an atmosphere in which your son can grow in these three areas just as Jesus did.

Growth in wisdom. The Greek word for "grew" is *prokopto.* While it is often translated in its sense of forward movement, progress, or increase (KJV), it also encompasses the more forceful idea of advancing as if by beating. In Luke 2:52, this word is used in the imperfect tense, which means the action is continual or repeated. In both sense and tense then, the word is not passive. It is a powerful and insistent process. *Sophia,* the Greek word for wisdom, carries the idea of both worldly and spiritual insight. So, when you are nurturing the "growth in wisdom" area of your son's life, you are deliberately focusing him so he can make good judgments relating to God and relating to the world around him. You are feeding into his emotional stability. A son with clear insight exhibits balanced emotions and is therefore wise. Growth in wisdom, then, is the driven, profitable, and positive maturation of your son's ability to handle his emotional responses to God and to the world around him, accomplished only by consistent nurturing and, yes, sometimes prodding. Jesus exhibited clear insight and balanced emotions as he questioned the leaders in the temple.

Begin nurturing this growth in wisdom almost as soon as the child exits the womb. I remember my infant boys' "experiment" with biting down on my breasts while they were nursing. A slight pluck on their tiny cheeks and a stern look down into their little eyes moved them to increase in wisdom and not do that again. It was good judgment on their part to cease and desist from causing pain to the one who was their source of life-sustaining nourishment.

I continued such training in wisdom with them at two years of age when I wouldn't allow them to wreak havoc in a Sunday school class, disturbing the teacher who was trying to plant a spiritual lesson into them; and with them at five years of age when I insisted they play nicely with other children on the kindergarten playground beside whom they would have to work once back in the classroom. Our sons will continue to grow in wisdom as we consistently point them toward the good choices they should make by making the poor choices extremely uncomfortable.

Boys will become stunted in their wisdom growth if not deliberately pointed toward and expected to make positive decisions. And the only way they will know they have made an immature decision is if the consequences of that poor decision adequately cause them some sort of suffering. One reason boys with perfectly good minds continually fail year after year in school is because someone allows it and the pain of failure is not ramped up enough to hurt. Why should a sixteen-year-old young man fail courses in school and still attend school dances, play on the basketball team, or strut around with a cell phone and wear hundred-dollar sneakers?

The book of Proverbs has quite a bit to say about wise sons. You will know you are on the right track of raising a wise son when you see some of the following attributes or results.

"He who gathers crops in summer is a wise son, but he who sleeps during harvest is a disgraceful son" (Proverbs 10:5). Many of our sons know nothing at all about farming, but they can know about taking care of business and not procrastinating. Guide your son to get things done in a timely fashion. Place an analog clock in your preschooler's room and encourage him to complete tasks by the time the big hand moves from the three to the six. This will begin an understanding of the value of wise time management as well as teach him how to tell time. Help your son during his elementary years by carving out definite time slots for homework completion. Do not allow your middle-school-aged son to drag his feet as he crosses the street, and make it a priority for your high schooler to search for college scholarships throughout his high school years.

Step Aside

At whatever age your son is, observe the kinds of decisions he has to make. For one week, watch your reactions to his decision-making process. Do you find yourself making decisions for him? If so, consider how you can step back and revise your tactics. Try to move from making choices for him to helping him see which options are wise and which options are foolish.

In other words, throughout your son's life, help him to operate ahead of the curve rather than behind it.

If you have a personal problem with procrastination, now is as good a time as any for you to overcome that tendency yourself. Have you noticed that parenting requires us to check ourselves in many areas since we are expected to demonstrate what our sons should duplicate?

"A wise son heeds his father's instruction, but a mocker does not listen to rebuke" (Proverbs 13:1). I never cease to be amazed that teenage boys accept harsh instruction from their football coach but refuse to obey their mother's instructions at home or their teachers' instructions at school. Those football players know that the coach means business, and they will "ride the pine" if they don't tow the line. You see, those boys clearly know how far they can go with the coach before a painful consequence, such as warming the bench, ensues. They also know the coach is requiring all he requires of them for their own good, to make them better ball players.

A father performing his rightful role ought to have earned that same respect from his son to the point the boy heeds his father's instruction and receives rebuke with a good attitude. That type of relationship is nurtured when the boy knows the father has his best interest at heart and is only requiring that which will make him a better man. This point is also the basis of Ephesians 6:4, "Fathers, do not exasperate your children; instead, bring them up in the training and instruction of the Lord."

"He who keeps the law is a discerning son, but a companion of gluttons disgraces his father" (Proverbs 28:7). A wise son understands authority and knows the importance of obeying the law. I will talk about this more in chapter 8, but for now, remember this as a characteristic that your son won't practice unless you do.

"A wise son brings joy to his father, but a foolish son grief to his mother" (Proverbs 10:1), and *"A wise son brings joy to his father, but a foolish man despises his mother"* (Proverbs 15:20). Imagine a mother's tears and heartache when she receives a frantic call from her seventeen-year-old

son's girlfriend telling her that her boy is in the hospital battling for his life after being shot in a fight. Her panic mingles with grief when she discovers, to her chagrin, that her son is a gang member.

Just as it is heartbreaking to find your son has messed up, it is indeed a joy to watch your son make wise decisions. How proud I was when Mark returned home for a month's Christmas vacation after his first semester away at college and the second day he was home he was back at work at his old job. To spend some of his four-week vacation earning money was a wise choice that he made on his own. As his mother, I'm feeling no grief about that kind of decision.

Growth in Stature. Just as it is your job to take care of the emotional growth of your son, it is your job to take care of the physical needs of your son. This seems like it should go without saying, but since God mentions it, I will too. After all, the first things most new parents are concerned about are feeding, clothing, and housing our children. Some of us even put off childbearing until we feel we are in a good financial position to meet these basic needs.

The Greek word for "stature" is *helikia*, which encompasses maturity in both age and height. Your son's growth in years should correspond with his growth in size. In other words, if we want our sons to grow into Christ's image, we need to be concerned about their healthy mental growth as much as their healthy physical growth. Both areas are of equal importance. Nothing bothers you about the nonsensical babbling of your infant son as he crawls through the house. However, once that child starts walking, you expect him to start talking too. (True, you soon want him to sit down and be quiet, but that's another subject altogether.) The point is that mental acumen and physical growth should be naturally parallel. Children should not be pushed into adulthood but should be allowed to experience childhood. They will be grown-ups much longer than they will be children, and once they are grown, childhood can never be recaptured.

Carefully watch that your son's mind matures with his body. Don't let either run ahead of the other. For example, if you intend to take your son to the movies, pay attention to the ratings.

PG-13 and R ratings are usually applied to films that are most highly publicized and therefore are the most popular among kids. However, there are reasons why parental guidance for those under age thirteen is strongly suggested. Children aged twelve and under should not be exposed to the high levels of violence, adult themes, and raunchy language sometimes used in those films. Kids under twelve are not mentally mature enough to handle the thoughts that can form in their minds from seeing some of the images so vividly portrayed on the screen. Their minds still may not be fully able to separate reality from fantasy.

The R (Restricted) rating that blocks viewing to children under seventeen should be just as strictly enforced for the same reasons mentioned above. Think about it: if Hollywood has enough sense to tell you, "We're going to show some things and say some things your kids shouldn't see," shouldn't you be wise enough to pick up that message and heed it?

Conversely, if your son is eight years old and still cannot or will not prepare his own simple breakfast of cereal or toast with juice, something's wrong.

Step Aside

How old is your son? What can he do for himself that you are still doing for him?

Take a survey of some of your Christian friends who have boys you admire. Ask them questions like the following:

At what age did you allow your son to do certain things, such as dress himself, wash dishes, wash his own clothes, sleep over at a friend's house, ride the bus alone, get a job, etc.?

How did you know your son was ready for these responsibilities?

How did your son handle these new responsibilities?

While this is not a scientific survey, and I'm not suggesting that you take their word as gospel, positive parenting role models are many times a good gauge of what really works in raising kids.

Growth in Favor with God. You must also take care to provide an atmosphere in which your son's soul can prosper. The soul is the spiritual part of a person that shines through in his or her words and actions. If your son's soul is healthy, his words and actions will bear that out. Your role in nurturing his soul is to promote the healthy growth of his relationship with the Lord and his relationships with others around him.

Do you remember the Sunday school song "If You're Happy and You Know It"? The words say:

> If you're happy and you know it,
> Then your face will surely show it,
> If you're happy and you know it, clap your hands.

Successive verses say to stomp your feet, say amen, and do all three. When I was a child, I sang that song with great gusto because I was happy and I knew it. I could sing with such enthusiasm because my soul was healthy. I grew up in a household built on a foundation of belief in God, and we honored him. I never even considered the possibilities that God did not love me or was not real. Such assurance provided a balance in my life that made it easy for me to approach God for myself and to deepen my relationship with him as I matured.

The same will be true for your son as you raise him in an environment that honors God. The Greek word for "favor" or "grace"—*charis*—means "acceptable" or "of benefit." It is our job as parents to raise our sons to understand both what is acceptable to God and beneficial to others. A foundation of acceptance provides the balance your son will need to function well in both. When his relationship with God and his relationship to society properly coincide, the outcome will be ministry. That which is fundamentally true for him on the inside, down in his soul, will radiate to the outside, and he will relate well with others through his personality and through his ministry. In chapter 6, I will discuss further how you can help your son's personality shine and thereby help him to relate to others in ministry.

3
The Young Man Tempted on the Cusp of Ministry

Matthew 4:1-11

What do Michael Jordan and Condoleezza Rice have in common? They both made the choice to forgo things their friends had and did with a view to something grand in the future. While a sophomore at Emsley A. Laney High School just outside Wilmington, North Carolina, Michael Jordan, now known as the greatest basketball player of all time, actually got cut from the basketball team because he was only five-eleven. That next summer, instead of doing other activities, he practiced and practiced basketball, and surprisingly grew four inches. He made the team the next year and went on to average twenty-five points per game in his last two high school years. He was even selected to the McDonald's All-American Team as a senior.[1]

What about Condoleezza Rice, the sixty-sixth U.S. secretary of state? A woman doesn't rise to the top of the political heap by being mediocre, and her biography details her lifelong habit of concentrating on excellence. Besides her numerous achievements in education and politics, she is a virtuoso pianist. Early in childhood her parents recognized her exceptional aptitude for music. Her biography says that "at age four, she mastered a handful of pieces and gave her first recital. The intense focus on piano cut into her playtime, as did the other projects Angelena [her mother] set up for her. Condi spent more time indoors—practicing piano and French—than did most of the other girls on the block."2

Long before their emergence to the top of their fields, both Jordan and Rice had recognized a calling to be great. That calling was not an egotistical one; they were simply motivated to reach as high as they could with what God had given them. This motivation caused them to work hard and make quality choices all through their lives—choices that weren't always easy, many times involving sacrifice and solitude, and no doubt many times involving temptations to take an easier route.

We find that same inner drive in our Lord Jesus. As we saw in chapter 2, long before his emergence into ministry, his seriousness of purpose shone through in his intense questioning of the religious leaders in the temple. His recognition of his purpose was made clear in his statement to his frantic mother when he said, "Why were you searching for me? Didn't you know I had to be in my Father's house?" (Luke 2:49; KJV, "about my Father's business").

Years later, on the very cusp of his ministry, Jesus faced a temptation to skirt around that purpose of being about his Father's business. Since many temptations will pull at our sons as they journey toward conformity to the image of Christ, let's build into our sons the five principles we can glean from how Jesus successfully handled his temptation in Matthew 4:1-11.

Principle One: Jesus Was Led by the Spirit

Matthew 4:1 tells us that "Jesus was led by the Spirit into the desert to be tempted by the devil." Three things jump out at me from this one statement, the most poignant being the fact that Jesus was led by the Spirit. To be led by the Spirit, he had to be familiar with the voice of the Spirit. It may seem obvious, but it still bears mentioning that we are familiar with that with which we spend our time. Why do you think you can still sing the lyrics and mimic the bass lines and guitar runs from a top-40 song that was popular thirty years ago? You can do that because of familiarity. You spent countless hours listening to, singing, and dancing to that song.

When familiarity breeds action, we call it instinct. We instinctively do that which is inbred in us to do. Because of practice, exposure, and experience, I throw my arm in front of the person riding in the passenger seat when I must suddenly hit the brakes while I'm driving. Even now in their teen years, instinctively I stop to listen when one of my sons is coughing in another room. I'm ready to go handle the trouble if the coughing doesn't stop.

Like Jesus and other biblical men, our sons can instinctively tune their ears to and become familiar with God's voice. Their "hearing" will become more and more acute—instinctual—with practice, exposure, and experience.

"So how," you ask, "do I begin to build in my son instinctual responses to the Spirit of God?" Perhaps you could start building the practice of listening to God's voice by helping your son search the Scriptures for God's thoughts about what he wants to do. For example, let's say your son wants to read a book about witchcraft. Ask him, "Does God's Word have anything to say about witchcraft? If so, what? Based on what God's Word says, do you think reading the book would be okay with God?" Don't overkill this idea with every little decision, such as which tennis shoes to wear. But if you make it a habit to see what God has to say even before you give a parental answer, you will begin building in your son the practice of listening to God's voice.

Your sons can also get used to hearing God's voice through exposure to others who hear God's voice—friends, family, and church members who have a track record of relying on God's guidance to make decisions. People who listen to God's leading may not have perfect lives, but they have lives that reveal God's blessings. God clearly blesses those who listen to his voice. Look at what God promised to do for the people of Israel if they would just allow God to direct them:

> Then the LORD your God will make you most prosperous in all the work of your hands and in the fruit of your womb, the young of your livestock and the crops of your land. The LORD will again delight in you and make you prosperous, just as he delighted in your fathers, if you obey the LORD your God and keep his commands and decrees that are written in this Book of the Law and turn to the LORD your God with all your heart and with all your soul. (Deuteronomy 30:9-10)

Your son will probably best learn God's voice through experience. A time will come when you can't help him hear from God. As one of God's children, he eventually will hear God's voice for himself.

I really wanted Matthew to attend Biola University, a stellar Christian university, but he desired so strongly to attend the University of Southern California that he practically bled their cardinal and gold school colors. Both schools had film programs. USC's was better established, but Biola's was steadily on the rise. Knowing the challenges he would face as he entered the business of Hollywood, I wanted Matthew to have an even stronger Christian foundation than the one we had given him at home. After having spent two years as a student myself on each campus, I knew Biola could meet that criterion when USC simply could and would not.

However, as I said, Matthew was determined to attend USC. He was accepted to both schools among others. He visited both campuses and spoke with people connected to the film departments; then he said no more for several months about his decision. As his high school graduation date drew closer, my anticipation about his selection grew. I knew the graduates' college acceptances and choices would be announced during the commencement ceremony. Finally, Matthew told me he had chosen Biola.

I was elated but surprised, so I had to find out what had happened. "Matthew," I asked, "I know how much you wanted to become a USC Trojan. What changed your mind?"

His answer is one I'll never forget. He said, "I prayed about it, Mom." Matthew had allowed the voice of God to change both his mind and his desire. The many open doors along his career path that have presented themselves to him while at Biola is continual confirmation that his choice was indeed directed by God.

The second thing that jumps out at me from Matthew 4:1 is that Jesus didn't question where the Spirit led him, even though the desert was not a pleasant place. I remember attending a missionary conference and sincerely asking the Lord not to send me onto the mission field in a third world country. That probably sounds very unholy, but I believe in being up front and honest with God in prayer; I'm just not cut out for "roughing it." Thankfully the Lord has allowed me to support missions from the sidelines while using my gifts to serve others here at home.

All of us, our sons included, must operate at our highest potential wherever the Spirit specifically leads. Proverbs 22:6 says, "Train a child in the way he should go,

Step Aside

Build in your son instinctual responses to the Spirit of God.

By practice. The next time your son asks for permission to do something new, practice listening to God's voice by searching the Scriptures for God's thoughts about the request.

By exposure. Have your son conduct a short survey of at least three Christians you know who rely on God to make decisions. Ask the people to explain the decision they had to make, their alternatives, and how they knew what God was telling them to do.

By experience. Encourage your son to pray about the decisions he has to make and then wait to hear from God through the Scriptures, the wisdom of a Christian mentor, and/or his own peace about his decision.

and when he is old he will not turn from it." Our job as parents is to lead our sons toward that which God has placed inside of them. This means we must know them well, and I will talk more about that in chapter 7. Suffice it to say for now that guidance based on an understanding of God's purpose for our children clears the spiritual airwaves so that our boys can clearly hear where God wants them to go in life.

We want our sons to be as attuned to the voice of God as was Abram. We are told in Genesis 12:1 that the Lord told Abram, "Leave your country, your people and your father's household and go to the land I will show you." Now that required faith in the voice of God. When God told Abram to leave his home, he didn't tell him exactly where he was going, just to "the land I will show you." Imagine Abram's wife Sarai's surprise when he came into the tent with that news. Nevertheless, Abram (later Abraham) ended up being the great-grandfather of the patriarchs of the twelve tribes of Israel who were ultimately to live in that land God showed him. He did the uncomfortable in the present for a better future.

The third thing that jumps out at me from Matthew 4:1 is that Jesus didn't question what the Spirit led him to experience, even though he had to face the devil himself. Many times we bristle, not only about where we are asked to go, but more frequently about what we are asked to do. Noah had a steady relationship with the Lord and found grace in God's eyes when God despaired of humankind's wickedness. Noah knew God's voice, and although he may not have known what an ark was or even what rain was, he followed God's precise directions to build an ark for the saving of his family and all the land animals (see Genesis 6–9).

Let your son know that God's voice can always be trusted, and that the end result of obedience to it is always good.

Step Aside

Encourage your son to bloom where he is planted, especially if he is in a place he doesn't want to be, such as at a certain school or on a losing sports team.

Abraham traveled through the beautiful land God promised to him and his ancestors. Noah's whole family was saved through the flood and lived to start building the population again. Job, another Old Testament figure, lost everything—family, wealth, and health—but he hung in there with God and was restored double for his trouble (see Job 1–2; 40–42).

God's voice, heard in the Bible's commandments and instructions, is always for our good. You can help your son appreciate God's Word by showing him how much freedom he has as a Christian, rather than always using God's Word as something restrictive. For example, when discussing the fact that stealing is wrong, point out all the great things about not stealing. You can be proud of your purchases, having saved up your hard-earned money to obtain the item. You can walk in and out of stores guilt-free. You avoid nasty encounters with the police, juvenile hall, and possibly prison!

Principle Two: Jesus Separated Himself from Some Physical Gratifications

Matthew 4:2 tells us that Jesus had been fasting forty days and forty nights, and at the end of the fast, he was hungry. This incident follows Jesus' baptism by John and confirmation from God himself that Jesus was to be listened to and followed (see Matthew 3).

Why is this principle applicable to our sons? Matthew Henry, commenting on the present passage, had the following thoughts: "After we have been admitted into the communion

Step Aside

Take two or three commandments (Exodus 20:1-17) or any other biblical instructions of your choice that are given in the negative (e.g., "You shall not steal"). Have your son consider that commandment or instruction and then write out at least three things he can do based on that verse. See the above paragraph about stealing for an example.

of God, we must expect to be set upon by Satan. The enriched soul must double its guard. . . . The Devil has a particular spite at useful persons, who are not only good, but given to do good, especially at their first setting out."[3]

You are reading this book because you already see your son as an "enriched soul." Following the leading of the Spirit will require him to separate himself from some of the physical gratifications that everyone else seems to be enjoying, because Satan is looking for opportunities to involve him in activities that could destroy his witness. Now this one is tough. It is easy to tell your son no and make that stick because you're in charge, but how do you motivate a kid to forgo, on his own, doing things that look like fun? How do you move that kind of motivation from head to heart?

The answer begins in the trust factor that you build between you and your son. Never lie to him. He must be able to see you as an honest, dependable individual whose word can be trusted. When this factor is in place, you can reason with your son about the probable positive and negative consequences of his choices. Even when he has to do without things his friends have or miss out on things his friends are doing, he will have an inner conviction that you have his best interest at heart.

I refused to buy in-line skates for Mark, my youngest son. His aunt Terri, a pediatric nurse at the time, told us of the many children admitted to the hospital with ankle injuries as a result of using in-line skates. Mark had his hopes set on playing college and professional basketball, and I knew the importance of strong ankles for that game, so that was the reason for my injunction. I found out that Mark skated with friends from time to time when not at home with me, so he didn't internalize my protective caution. I reiterated my reasoning to him and then placed the responsibility for care for his ankles on him. He spent considerably less time skating than many of his friends and thankfully avoided injury. He is now glad his ankles are strong.

We also prohibited our boys from wearing pierced earrings and tattoos. Their dad made the point that securing professional jobs requires a professional look, and earrings and tattoos could shut them out of certain career opportunities they may want in the future. Mark pierced his own ear, but that didn't do him much good, because as long as he lived at home, he was not allowed to wear an earring. The funny thing is, now that he is in college, we still don't see the earring.

Start with little, practical things to begin to build the principle of denial of physical gratification. As your son matures, you can discuss weightier matters, such as refraining from alcohol and drug use and abstaining from sexual activity until marriage.

Principle Three: Jesus Recognized the Importance of God's Word

We can see the esteem with which Jesus held God's Word exemplified in his encounter with Satan after his forty days of fasting. When the tempter came to him and said, "If you are the Son of God, tell these stones to become bread," Jesus answered, "It is written: 'Man does not live on bread alone, but on every word that comes from the mouth of God'" (Matthew 4:3-4). In Job 23:12, the Old Testament figure expressed the same sentiment this way: "I have not departed from the commands of his lips; I have treasured the words of his mouth more than my daily bread."

Jesus teaches us here to allow God to fulfill our needs rather than try to fulfill them on our own. The most effective way to teach this principle to our sons is by living its truth. When was the last time your son heard you ask God to meet your daily needs or to fulfill the desires of your heart? Then when was the

Step Aside
■ List activities in which your son wants to participate.

■ Set your household policy as to whether you will allow your son to participate in each activity, and then stick to it. God's Word, your son's age, and his ability to understand your decision will determine how you approach the explanation of your choice.

last time your son watched you wait until God answered rather than maneuver to make things work out for yourself? I'll talk more in chapter 5 about prayer and Bible study, but make a mental note here of the level of dependence Jesus placed in God's Word.

Principle Four: Jesus Existed to Do God's Will, Not the Other Way Around

Matthew 4:5-7 gives us the story:

> Then the devil took him to the holy city and had him stand on the highest point of the temple. "If you are the Son of God," he said, "throw yourself down. For it is written:
>
>> "'He will command his angels concerning you,
>> and they will lift you up in their hands,
>> so that you will not strike your foot against a stone.'"
>
> Jesus answered him, "It is also written: 'Do not put the Lord your God to the test.'"

You see, Satan was trying to drive Jesus to make God prove himself. This was the essence of Satan's rebellious act that got him thrown out of heaven. When as Lucifer he tried to place his throne above God's, he was essentially saying, "Okay God, let's see what you've got. Do you have what it takes to keep your power? Bring it on." If Jesus had fallen for this temptation, he would have been treating God the same way. In other words, Jesus would be concentrating on himself rather than on God.

Trying to force the God of the universe to prove himself to you is an act of rebellion, and you end up on the losing end. Our sons can learn from this principle that it is not necessary to require that God perform some fantastic feat to be God. God is God without help from us. Indeed, God can perform some fantastic feats, but they are carried out at his discretion, not ours.

To counteract this temptation to try to force God to prove himself, we can raise our sons to understand they are not the center of the universe; instead, they exist to serve God. This may be a difficult principle to teach, especially for a single mother who has come to rely on her son as the "man of the house." Boys treated in this manner can become self-absorbed, looking for everyone in their lives to treat them with the same deference they have always received from their mother. What a rude awakening these boys are set up to receive when they do venture out of Mother's house and into the real world where they will be expected to fend for themselves.

Mrs. Garvin treated her son this way. Alex was a strapping fifteen-year-old when I met him. He was built like a linebacker, and our school's football team was excited to welcome him to the student body. The only problem was that Alex had serious procrastination issues, and it became evident early in his career at our school that his mother had a habit of making excuses for him. She was the reason he kept moving from school to school. Instead of accepting the painful reality that her son was undisciplined and dysfunctional, she transferred the blame to the school and made the excuse that no educational institution was in tune with his needs. When Alex's procrastination got the best of him again and she couldn't talk our instructors into giving him grades he didn't deserve, Mrs. Garvin withdrew him and moved him once again to another school. The last we heard, Alex had failed to graduate with his class, was still living at home, and was floundering around from job to job while trying to earn his GED through a community college program.

My friend Diana works in the registrar's office at a community college. She sees a lot of mothers bringing in their sons to make up work they have blown off in high school. She told me she can tell the ones who have been enabled in their bad habits by their mothers over the years. The mother approaches the counter carrying the boy's identification in her purse and intending to fill out the paperwork for him. Diana immediately tries to turn the tables by addressing the young man, thus encouraging him to take responsibility for enrollment in the classes he must take. For some, Diana can tell this is the first time both mother and son have been confronted with the reality that he has to face the music of his own inadequacies.

One particular appointment with a mother-son team shocked Diana and changed her perspective on raising her own sons. She looked up from her desk to see an eighty-year-old woman asking for registration materials for her sixty-year-old son who was standing behind her. This elderly man had never been independent, and now, as his mother faced declining health, she wanted to get him enrolled in school and onto a path toward taking care of himself before she died. Diana witnessed an extreme example of what can happen to a man who is catered to by his mother his entire life. She was awakened to the seriousness of imparting independence to her own two young sons.

Communicating principle four to our sons that they exist to do God's will, not the other way around, will happen as we do two things. First parents, especially mothers, must build our sons' self-esteem without causing them to think they are the center of the universe. Guide them as they grow up and face and tackle their own inadequacies. Second, we must help our sons serve God rather than expect God to work for them. Instead of focusing on how God is supposed to bless them, they will begin to see that God is at work as they serve others.

I heard a woman on Christian radio talking about how her children serve others at Christmastime. Instead of giving gifts to each other, they spend their money fulfilling the Christmas wishes of the children in a needy family. The first year they did this, she had to do some convincing, but once her kids witnessed the smiles and

Step Aside

■ Are you making excuses for some aspect of your son's behavior rather than addressing his behavior head-on?

■ If so, list the behaviors for which you make excuses.

■ Write a plan for how you and your son will deal with the behavior that needs to be changed.

thankfulness of the other family, they took to the project whole-heartedly and have made their giving an annual tradition.

Principle Five: Jesus Recognized That Satan Was Demanding Worship

The final temptation Jesus faced in this passage as he was on the cusp of his ministry dealt with who would receive worship.

> Again, the devil took him to a very high mountain and showed him all the kingdoms of the world and their splendor. "All this I will give you," he said, "if you will bow down and worship me."
> Jesus said to him, "Away from me, Satan! For it is written: 'Worship the Lord your God, and serve him only.'" (Matthew 4:8-10)

Jesus didn't fall for the trick. Satan not only tried to get Jesus to challenge God's power, but he tried to divert Jesus' worship as well. Thankfully, Jesus refused to give Satan the worship he was demanding.

When our sons sin, they are obeying Satan and thereby worshiping him. Romans 6:16 makes this clear: "Don't you know that when you offer yourselves to someone to obey him as slaves, you are slaves to the one whom you obey—whether you are slaves to sin, which leads to death, or to obedience, which leads to righteousness?" Our boys, therefore, need to be able to discern what voices are the right voices to obey.

How do we help our boys in this area? First, constantly impart wisdom to your sons. Get your answers from the Word of God; then relate those answers to the situations of your sons' lives. Let your sons know that you know what you are talking about. Second, surround your sons with people from whom they can also hear wisdom. Third, point out the types of people who are not trustworthy. Let your son see those who are in negative situations because of their own poor choices or because of following bad advice. Perhaps if we expose our boys to these people through our own conversations, they will be less likely to be caught up in negative or dangerous situations because of following or listening to them.

Even with our diligence carrying out the above three directives, boys still will sometimes listen to the wrong people. Keep the lines of communication clear and your eyes open so you can contradict bad advice as soon as possible and hopefully shut down any adverse consequences that might ensue as a result of your son's heeding of that advice.

Sometimes we are so busy teaching our sons to be kind and polite that we neglect to teach them how and why to say no. Exercising discernment involves knowing when to say no decisively. Jesus knew to say no decisively to Satan. We can turn to the Word of God to teach this skill to our boys in the way we deal with providing permission to them. Let me explain.

I try to base my reasons for everything I do on the Word of God, so that carries over into child rearing. If the Bible says something is wrong, then there is a rule in my house against it. On the other hand, if God sees nothing wrong with doing something, why should I? If there is no precept or principle in the Bible relating to an issue, why sweat it? So I apply four checkpoints to determine whether I should say yes or no to something.

First, *is it immoral?* The first question to ask when considering a decision is whether there is a clear scriptural injunction against what is being requested. Second, *is it illegal?* Will carry-

Step Aside

- Can you identify anything that is exalting itself against God in your son's life? Think about things like participating in sports games on Sundays, viewing or listening to certain types of entertainment (music, movies, literature, etc.), or being asked to take certain oaths to join clubs or fraternities.

- What can you do to eliminate anything in your son's life that is stealing worship from God?

ing out this request break any laws? If so, the answer to the request is obviously no. Third, *is it injurious?* Would it be dangerous for the boys to have or do whatever they're requesting? Finally, *is it improper?* My final consideration concerns the social acceptability of granting a request.

These same checkpoints can be used to help our sons discern whether the voice they are hearing is a wise one to follow. When confronted with a choice or suggestion, teach them to quickly run through the checklist: is it immoral, illegal, injurious, or improper? If the answer to any one is yes, their answer must be a decisive no.

These checkpoints can help your son know how to pick his battles. For example, when my nephew Eric was in middle school, he received a poor grade in English one semester because he refused to do the literature assignment in which his public school teacher required the students to create a god during their study of Greek mythology. Eric had judged the assignment as immoral and improper based on what he had learned in Sunday school about one of the Ten Commandments. To him, following that assignment would be like making an idol, and he was having none of that.

NOTES

1. Michael Jordan biography, http://www.imdb.com/name/nm0003044/bio.

2. Antonia Felix, *Condi: The Condoleezza Rice Story* (New York: Newmarket, 2005), 41.

3. Matthew Henry, *Matthew Henry's Commentary on the Whole Bible* 1706), http://www.studylight.org/com/mhc-com/view.cgi?book=mt&chapter=4&verse=2#mt4_2.

4
The Grown Son at the Wedding at Cana

John 2:1-11

When I sat down to write this chapter, I was facing the very juncture in my own life about which I was writing. Mark would be graduating from high school in a couple of months and leaving home for college. Matthew had left two years earlier, and even with his university being only twenty minutes away from our home, he lived on campus and we rarely saw him. He was building his own life and was absorbed in his own interests. He didn't even come home for the summer, opting to live with his aunt whose home was closer to his summer internship job.

I was feeling a little more angst about Mark's departure than I had felt about Matthew's. He was my last child. My employment in the boys' upbringing had lasted for the past twenty years, and the hands-on part of that job would soon come to an abrupt end. But that is the whole idea. I knew when I took the job that I would be working my way out of it. That was the reason for all the previous chapters of this book—to set up both my children and me for the day the roles would change, the day they would separate from my parental control and be able to successfully control themselves.

We see this transition happen in the life of Jesus the day he attended a wedding in a little town called Cana (see John 2:1-11).

From this story, we learn three important lessons about letting our sons go. So although it may be uncomfortable and a little disquieting, let's consider the issues of *separation*, *subordination*, and *limitation*.

Lesson One: Separation

In contrast to the twenty years I had spent molding my boys, Mary had spent thirty mothering her eldest Son. Jesus' public ministry had not yet launched, but here at thirty years old, he had begun communicating with some men who would become known as his disciples. We take up the story of Mary, Jesus, and his disciples at a wedding where they become aware of a problem.

> On the third day [after John's preaching, Jesus' baptism, and Jesus' starting to choose his disciples] a wedding took place at Cana in Galilee. Jesus' mother was there, and Jesus and his disciples had also been invited to the wedding. When the wine was gone, Jesus' mother said to him, "They have no more wine."
>
> "Dear woman, why do you involve me?" Jesus replied. "My time has not yet come." (John 2:1-3)

This passage suggests a close relationship between Jesus and his mother. Bible scholars speculate that Joseph, Jesus' earthly father, had probably died by this time in Jesus' life, because we don't hear of him any more once Jesus becomes an adult. If this was the case, as the eldest son, Jesus would have taken the role of head of the home. Mary understandably would have been used to turning to him when she needed a problem solved.

This time Mary's request was met with an unusual response. When she alerted Jesus that there was no more wine, his response was, "My time has not yet come." Mary had overstepped her bounds in regard to what she was asking him to do. His response was a revelation to her that it was time for him to move out of the relationship to which they had become accustomed.

Moms, a day will come when your son will have to do the same thing. When your son becomes a man, your relationship with him will change. He needs to move, and you need to let him move, into that new relationship. It is interesting that this juncture happened for Jesus and Mary at a wedding, because that is when we usually think of it happening. We think our influence will ultimately be replaced by that of our son's wife. After all, the Bible tells us that when a man marries, he should leave his father and mother and be united to his wife (see Genesis 2:24). Although Jesus never married, he did mature and leave his childhood home. So will your son.

Mature sons need their own space. Let them go away to college or the military. Let them move into their own homes with their own dishes to wash, toilets to clean, and light bills to pay. Your son's future wife will not get what she needs if you give her a grown male body that's housing a little boy's mentality. Nothing is worse than a man who thinks his wife is supposed to be his mother. And a woman who raises a boy to be a man eventually won't want him to be *her* man, because she will always see him as the one she raised. Mature sons need to leave their mothers in terms of both influence and dependence.

An example of healthy attachment is a phone call at 11:00 p.m. from your college-freshman son who is feeling a homesick pang at his first final exam time. You talk for a while until he feels better, he hangs up and returns to his studies, and you go to bed. Unhealthy attachment is when that same son makes that same phone call, but instead of talking him through his trouble, you hop on the first plane, train, or automobile to get to him with chocolate chip cookies and milk.

Step Aside

What are you doing to keep your son attached to you?

If you had an answer above, how might you need to change your approach?

Unhealthy attachments block your son from experiencing the opportunity of working out his own problems at his maturity level. Your two-year-old needs you to hold his hand or hug him when the doctor gives him a shot; your seventeen-year-old can take himself to the doctor. Get the idea?

Lesson Two: Subordination

In terms of influence, sons may separate physically from their mothers, but some mothers still like to exert psychological and emotional control over their boys. The second lesson Jesus teaches us here has to do with the need for a son to break free from being subordinate to his mother. Mature sons must take on their own responsibilities.

A television commercial illustrates this point. A middle-aged man stands in the living room with his coat on and luggage in both hands. He is sternly telling someone he has to leave. When the camera shot widens, we see that he is talking to his mother. She stands with her back to him, expressionless. Suddenly she turns to him smiling and nodding her agreement with his plan to depart. In her hands, however, is a platter holding a scrumptious roast. When the son sees the food, he immediately drops his bags and rushes to the table. In the parting shot, he is still asserting that one day he is going to have to leave, and the mother is again nodding her agreement, obviously pleased that she has influenced her son to remain with her.

That particular commercial claims to be touting the power of a good meal, but it is saying so much more. It is showing the underhanded psychological influence many mothers insist on holding over their sons.

For centuries mothers have tried to hold on to their sons way past the time when those sons should be moving on into their own adult lives. This phenomenon still exists today. On February 1, 2005, the BBC online news reported that Italian men live with their mothers well into their thirties. A TV program backed up this story, saying that these men's mothers still mothered them literally: cleaning their rooms, cooking their meals, washing their clothes. The article says:

The proportion of Italians aged between 30 and 34 still living at home has doubled to well over a quarter, a recent
government report concludes. Sons linger even longer than
daughters, the government says, with 36.5% of men aged
30 to 34 remaining at home, compared to just 18.1% of
women. The numbers seem to feed the idea of Italian sons
so dependent on their mothers that they just cannot bear to
leave the maternal home. [These] men have become known
as "mammoni" in Italy.[1]

Verses 5-8 of our passage says:

His mother said to the servants, "Do whatever he tells
you."
Nearby stood six stone water jars, the kind used by the
Jews for ceremonial washing, each holding from twenty to
thirty gallons.
Jesus said to the servants, "Fill the jars with water"; so
they filled them to the brim.
Then he told them, "Now draw some out and take it to
the master of the banquet."
They did so.

Jesus was a grown man. Even after he told his mother that his
time had not yet come, she expected him to do something about the
wine situation. Look at Jesus' next action: he honored his mother's
wishes, but he honored them on his terms. Mary did not tell him
how to do what he was about to do. Although Scripture doesn't
address this, I believe the lack of specific instruction is important for
us to note. A significant transition in a mother's relationship with
her adult Son took place. Before now Jesus had obediently submitted to what she said, doing things the way she said to do them. Now
he gave her a little nudge with his words, and she left the results up
to him. As an adult, he was not self-centered, taking the attitude,

"I'm grown now, so what you have to say, Mom, is not important." Rather, he still honored what was important to his mother but gently let her know he had to do things his way now.

If our relationship with our sons is what it should be, we will let them move into their own sphere of responsibility without fear. In turn, they will maintain respect for those who fed into their lives, especially their mothers. Why do you think Mother's Day is one of the biggest holidays of the year? A mother's love will always be honored, respected, remembered, and admired, but a mother's ruling hands must drop the gavel and director's baton and fold in prayer for this son who is now shouldering his own adult responsibilities.

I will always be proud of my nephew, Danny. After graduation from high school, he was accepted to Ohio State University on federal aid with a plan to study zoology. Well, those college science courses were a little harder than he expected, and he ended up unable to handle them. He lost his federal aid and his place in the program. His next move is what made me proud.

Danny did not run home to his mommy. He found a job working at a campus-operated hotel. He rented a bachelor apartment and rode back and forth to work on his bicycle—yes, that's right, in Ohio, sometimes in the snow! He began to really like the hotel business and took up courses at Columbus State Community College to work his way back into the university. He successfully returned to Ohio State and graduated with a degree in hospitality management.

Now my sister, Danny's mother, could have easily told him to come on home to California where he'd have a place to live, familiar surroundings, and family and friends for support. But she let Danny take the responsibility for himself as a young adult and work it out. Danny is now married with two children, a lovely home, and a career he loves in hotel management with a major hotel chain.

We raise our sons in Jesus' image when we allow them to take on responsibilities appropriate for their age. This is especially true of young adult sons, but we can start getting into practice at any age as our sons mature.

■ Do you instruct your toddler to pick up his own toys then hold him accountable if he forgets?

■ Do you mandate that your child eat the balanced diet you provide, and if he doesn't want to eat that, do you realize that he really isn't hungry? (A hungry child eats what is placed before him.)

■ Do you expect your child to bring notes home from his teacher and not tolerate his supposed "forgetfulness"?

■ Is your son expected to earn the "extras" like new toys, pricey clothing or shoes, electronics, and so on?

■ Do you hold your son to a standard concerning what grades in school you expect from him; then, if that standard is not met, do you take privileges away until he raises low grades?

These are just a few of the many things you can take a look at when helping your son to grow into a responsible adult. If he learns how to handle these small responsibilities, he will be better equipped to handle weightier matters, such as paying bills on time, driving carefully, showing up to work consistently and on time, taking care of his health, and providing for his family.

In our biblical passage, Jesus' mother may have pointed out the problem, but it was Jesus who took on the responsibility to handle the situation. It was his decision, not Mary's, to have the water pots filled with water so he could have something to work with. It was his word, not Mary's that the servants followed.

Your son can make decisions. Realize, too, that even if he does nothing, he has made a decision. The only way your son will mature in this area is if you let him make decisions and then let him either enjoy the outcome or suffer the consequences. Start when he is small by giving him choices that lead to limited negative circumstances if he chooses unwisely. For example, on a slightly cool day, let him be a little uncomfortable because of his decision to wear his sandals instead of his tennis shoes with thick, warm socks. As he grows older, the rewards and consequences related to his responsibilities should be both age-appropriate and sufficiently commensurate with the responsibilities.

Lesson Three: Limitation

Maturity in terms of independence begins to happen as we teach our sons to set their own limits, establish their own boundaries, and select their own level of excellence.

Setting Limits and Establishing Boundaries Limits deal with amount, speed, and distance. The limits your son sets will tell him how much is too much, how fast is too fast, and how far is too far. The boundaries he erects will be for his protection.

Although Mary discovered the wine shortage and told Jesus about it, the time had come for him to make his own decisions and set his own limits on how he would handle situations. In this case, Jesus set a limit that gently told Mary this was it on telling him what to do. Jesus handled the situation as he handled every other situation from then on—by meeting the need. The host had run out of wine, so Jesus made wine out of what the host did have—water.

You will know your son is maturing when he sets limits and establishes boundaries based on what he knows must be done. He will do what is necessary, regardless of his personal comfort level. He will curb his own freedom based on what he knows he has to do.

I remember my mother telling the story of how responsible my brother was at age sixteen when he first got his driver's license. Driving a car without an adult driver riding along is one of the first huge responsibilities your son will face. Nick passed his tests and was allowed to use our dad's car to go out with his three buddies. As Nick drove, his friends started clowning

> **Step Aside**
> What responsibilities do you carry that should be your son's?
>
> What are you going to do to delegate these responsibilities to him?

53

around in the car. Rather than join in like he usually did, Nick pulled the car over to the curb. When his friends noticed the car had stopped but they hadn't yet reached their destination, they wanted to know what was going on. Nick told them, in no uncertain terms, that he was responsible for his dad's car and they would have to stop playing around. He had no intention of wrecking the car because they couldn't wait to get where they were going before they got deep into playing around. His ultimatum was, "Pipe down or get out."

Nick could have lost face with his friends, and at sixteen that is a major concern; however, he moved beyond his own comfort zone and set the responsible limit.

You will never know if your son can set his own limits until you give him the opportunity to take on his own responsibility. Give him graduated levels of responsibility so that by the time he turns eighteen he will have had practice being responsible, knowing that every decision will reap some sort of consequence—good or bad.

Mark proved his ability to establish a boundary for himself soon after he received his driver's license and had his first car. One day he left early for a breakfast date, and I hadn't seen him all day. At 8:30 p.m. my cell phone rang. It was Mark telling me that after his date he'd spent the day with his buddy Camron and was having dinner at Camron's house. "I love you, Mom," he said, "and I didn't want you to worry about where I was or if I was okay." Although I had not given him a curfew, he established a boundary in his own mind concerning the time he had been away from home and called in when he realized he had been gone for quite a while.

I have read news reports about young adults overdoing it with drinking and partying once they move away to college. The sudden onslaught of freedom overrides their good sense. When Mommy and Daddy aren't enforcing rules anymore, these kids seem unable to rein themselves in. Their recklessness may have had its beginning with their parents' failure to let them suffer the consequences of their poor choices in the past. In an effort to protect them and keep them happy, perhaps their parents never allowed them to reap any negativity from what they sowed.

I see this every year at the high school where I teach. Certain students clown around for three years, never taking their education seriously. We keep the parents informed of the consistent poor grades, and we schedule meetings and workshops with the guidance/college counselor. We warn, provide extra help, volunteer additional hours, and suggest summer school—all to no avail. Then the senior year hits. We suddenly hear from "concerned" parents wondering what they can do to enable their children to graduate with their class.

Too little, too late. Those kids should have been kicked in the pants three years earlier, and now the parents are taking on the children's responsibility. Obviously, getting an education hasn't been important enough to the teens for them to take it seriously; why is it now a crisis and the parents are wringing their hands? The fact is, having one's child fail to graduate is embarrassing, and in these cases, clearly more so to the parents than to the children. Had these kids been allowed to suffer the consequences of their low grades early in their high school career (e.g., missing vacation because of summer school or not playing on the sophomore basketball team), they probably would have caught the vision for themselves about the importance of their education. Then they would have taken the responsibility upon themselves to get good grades and not even come close to the possibility of missing out on wearing the funny hat and gliding down the aisle to the strains of "Pomp and Circumstance."

Our sons will set their own boundaries only when the issues are important to them personally. Our job until they are grown is to train them, pointing them to issues about which they should care—their relationship with God, their concern for others, and a blameless reputation. When we see our boys establishing their own boundaries to protect these areas, we will know we have done our job.

Selecting His Own Level of Excellence The wine Jesus made in John 2:9-11 was excellent. He could have made any kind of wine he wanted; after all, he created the grapes! Not surprisingly, he made the best wine anyone had ever tasted. Mary knew her Son, and Jesus knew who he was and what he was capable of accomplishing. When we instill this same kind of self-knowledge in our sons, they too will rise to whatever occasion is at hand, but it is up to them to choose the level to which they will rise.

Our son Matthew is a filmmaker. He recognized his passion for this career early in his high school years and requested a video camera for a Christmas present. The line on the chart of his accomplishments in film has risen steadily ever since. We believed in his dream and supplied the first camera; then he took off believing in himself. By the time he was halfway through Biola University's film program, he had three award-winning films behind him and his fourth was in postproduction. Each film gets better.

We see that Jesus had a positive self-image by the assurance with which he approached every situation. Have you helped to instill a positive self-image in your son? If so, he will exhibit excellence on his own. He will have a pride in his own accomplishments apart from your prompting. He probably won't turn any water into wine, but you will begin to see him selecting his own level of excellence in other ways:

- Watch how he manages his appearance. He will keep his hair well groomed and his clothes clean and neat.
- Consider how he cares for his property, especially his car. A guy's car seems to be an extension of his personality. He will probably keep it up more fastidiously than he does his room.
- Pay attention to how he spends his money and uses credit. If you have taught him to be responsible, he will probably be careful with

his spending and saving, and he will take pains to maintain an excellent credit rating.

■ Watch how he gives of his time, talent, and treasure to the work of God's kingdom. Our maturing sons should never forget that their duty to God must always come first.

■ Watch his ability to manage his time wisely, not biting off more than he can chew or becoming a workaholic, but balancing his hours with work, leisure, and rest.

From watching Jesus' interaction with his mother at the wedding at Cana and learning the lessons connected to separation, subordination, and limitation, we will see that, like the Master, our sons will reveal through their actions who they really are on the inside. Verse 11 of our focal passage reads, "This, the first of his miraculous signs, Jesus performed at Cana in Galilee. He thus revealed his glory, and his disciples put their faith in him."

The decisions Jesus made and the solutions he implemented in times of crisis revealed who he was. His actions showed forth his glory. Likewise, your son must be allowed to become like Christ in his independence from you. Unlike the Savior, your son will make some mistakes and face the consequences as he matures, but that is to be expected of every human being. Just as lifting more weight than we normally lift grows great biceps and pectorals, and running farther than we normally run increases lung capacity, so exercising character builds character. Only as your son is allowed to push against resistance on his own will he develop tenacity and intestinal fortitude. Let go and watch him work through life's challenging situations. You may be surprised by, and you will certainly be proud of, how well he is able to handle the challenges that come his way.

NOTE
1. "Italians 'slow to leave the nest,'" BBC News, February 2005, http://news.bbc.co.uk/2/hi /europe/4227675.stm.

5
The Son in Relationship with His Father

We usually think of a habit as something negative, but the dictionary simply defines a habit as "an acquired behavior pattern regularly followed until it has become almost involuntary" and "a dominant or regular disposition or tendency; prevailing character or quality. Synonyms denote patterns of behavior established by continual repetition."[1] Aristotle said of habit, "We are what we repeatedly do. Excellence, then, is not an act, but a habit."[2]

In the excellent life of Jesus, his personal relationship with God, his Father, was defined by three habits: getting alone with God in prayer, relying on God's Word, and carrying out God's will. Jesus' relationship with his Father was sustained through prayer, proclaimed through use of the Word, and maintained through obedience.

Enough cannot be said about the importance of the relationship between a boy and his father. As many great fathers as there are, our country is nevertheless experiencing a fatherhood crisis that is seriously affecting the development of our boys.

According to the U.S. Census Bureau, 83.1 percent of single parents are mothers, and 26.1 percent of custodial single mothers and their children live in poverty.[3] In a *San Francisco Chronicle* article titled "Are Boys Better Off without Fathers?" Glenn Sacks wrote:

Numerous studies show that the rates of the four major youth pathologies—juvenile crime, teen pregnancy, teen drug abuse and school dropouts—are tightly correlated with fatherlessness. For example, a 1998 study published in the *Journal of Marriage and the Family* showed that even after controlling for all major socioeconomic factors, including income, teens not living with their fathers were twice as likely to abuse drugs as those living in intact, two-parent married families. Likewise, according to findings presented to the American Sociological Association in 1998, after eliminating all socioeconomic differences, boys who grew up outside of intact marriages were still more than twice as likely to end up in jail as those in intact homes.[4]

The fatherless crisis is even more tragic in the African American community. Census statistics indicate that almost half of all African American families have female heads of household.[5] Research presented in November 2006 by Linda Malone-Colon and Alex Roberts of the Center for Marriage and Families at the Institute for American Values says: "Family structure matters for young African American males. When African American boys live with two parents—especially their own two married parents—they typically enjoy greater economic security and better parenting. They also tend to have better health early on in life, better academic performance, and greater self-esteem. They are markedly less likely to be delinquent."[6]

Pastor Gillis Triplett of Atlanta has written extensively about the importance of fathers. He suggests that we must "unequivocally embrace these three critical truths: transitioning into manhood is not a natural process; it takes a man to raise a boy to be a man; and if boys aren't properly initiated into manhood, they are destined to embrace a subverted view of being a man."[7]

I realize that single mothers may be ready to turn me off now that I have quoted the point that it takes a man to raise a man. But think about this: we expect doctors to train medical interns, master teachers to train first-year teachers, and drill sergeants to train privates. Swimmers don't train chefs, accountants don't train ballerinas, and electricians don't train photographers. Why do we think men are not best capable of training boys to be men? Mothers can explain manhood, but fathers can model it.

Am I saying that sons of a single woman are lost if she doesn't have a man in her life? No, but I am saying it is up to a single mother to do her best to be sure her sons are exposed to Christian men who can serve as role models for them. But still, remember the central premise of this book: Jesus is the role model of manhood to whom we can point our sons. So, as you read this chapter, do not despair. Every point in this chapter can be carried out by the godly male father figures in your son's life, but when Christian men are unavailable, using the suggestions pointed out in this book, you can encourage your son to build his relationship with the one man who will indeed never leave him—the one man who can lead him positively at all times. Your son's strong relationship with Jesus will fill in the gaps and guide him toward strong manhood.

Lana became a single mother when her boys were upper-elementary age. It was important for her to remove them from the unhealthy household environment her home had become as a result of domestic violence, and correct the distorted view of manhood her boys had witnessed in their father. Lana was smart enough to realize, though, that if she had tried to directly counteract her husband's actions and attitudes, the boys could have internalized them in a subconscious act to protect their relationship with him. Her boys needed men in their lives whom they respected and who could model for them what manhood should be. Her single years were rough, but Lana determinedly focused her boys' eyes on Jesus, realizing that he was indeed their Savior in their current situation. If no man had stepped up, Jesus would have been sufficient; however, Lana continually reached out. Her brother, brother-in-law, pastor, and several friends' husbands pitched in to be her "village" until she married a wonderful man who stepped effectively into the fatherhood and manhood role her boys needed to see on a day-to-day basis.

Pastor Triplett presents some alarming statistics to emphasize the need for children to have a father in the home:

> It is no secret that fatherless homes account for 63% of youth suicides, 90% of homeless/runaway children, 85% of children with behavior problems, 71% of high school dropouts, 85% of youths in prison, 50% of teen mothers, [and] 80% of rapists motivated with displaced anger. . . . Get this point drilled in your mind; when boys are not properly indoctrinated into manhood, they are destined to embrace the subverted version of being a man. Subsequently, they'll exhibit some or all of these harrowing traits.
>
> 1. Shun marriage
> 2. Shun and mock education
> 3. Harbor deeply seated anger
> 4. Secretly question their manhood
> 5. Use and abuse the female gender
> 6. Become perpetual underachievers
> 7. Constantly seek instant gratification
> 8. Effortlessly abandon children they sire
> 9. Display glaring misogynistic tendencies
> 10. Mock God and embrace unrighteousness
> 11. Have no respect for their elders or authority
> 12. Embrace and glamorize the thug/criminal life
> 13. Eagerly commit crimes against their communities
> 14. Energetically subvert other males from true manhood[8]

Although Pastor Triplett's observances are mainly of African American boys, even a casual observance of teen culture easily bears out the horrifying reality that the above-mentioned mind-sets cross racial and ethnic lines. To raise our sons to be like Christ, we have to redeem their minds and hearts back from the societal viewpoints mentioned. My contention is that this will be done by encouraging them to mirror Jesus' close relationship with his Father as defined by the three habits Jesus exhibited: communicating with God in prayer, sharing God's Word, and carrying out God's will. When boys have a Christian father or father figure to confide in, that man's word to follow, and the drive to make that man proud, they will be well on their way to reflecting Christ's image.

Habit #1: Jesus sustained his relationship with his Father by communicating with him in prayer. Jesus had existed in eternity with God, so it makes sense that when he divested himself of his glory and came to earth, he would want to maintain close contact with his wonderful Father. Jesus deferred to his Father's direction, and God came through for his Son. That's a perfect example of the close connection that should exist between fathers and sons.

Even though our earthly relationships don't always operate as they should, the father and the son who are submitted to God and eager to make things work can build a strong foundation through communication. When lines of communication stay open, both sides grow. Understanding of and respect for each other are enhanced. This takes a concerted effort from both parties. The son must realize that his father's wisdom is worth considering, and the father must realize that his son—especially an older teen or young adult son—has some worthwhile ideas too.

Of course, a father has the greatest opportunity to make a significant impact on his son's life if he is involved as a godly father figure from the beginning. So dads, get yourselves together. Recognize the enormous responsibility you have to shape your sons' attitudes and beliefs. You will also have a profound influence on the development of his relationship with God. What your son understands about you as his father will shape his initial beliefs about God as his heavenly Father.

■ Do you demonstrate love for your son? God demonstrated his love for your son in that while he was still a sinner, Christ died for him (see Romans 5:8).

■ Do you provide for your son's physical needs? God tells your son not to worry about his food and clothing, because, as his Father, he has that covered (see Matthew 6:25-34).

■ Does your son know you will be there for him? God tells your son he will never leave nor forsake him (see Hebrews 13:5).

■ Does your son know he can trust your word? God tells your son that his words are exceedingly good for him (see Psalm 19:7-10).

Only you, Dad, can communicate what you want your son to know in the way you want him to know it. As your son matures, it is no one's duty but yours to communicate fatherhood and manhood to him.

Now, I understand that sometimes men have trouble talking to each other. They would rather gather around a basketball game or televised heavyweight boxing match and use lots of grunts than sit across a table and have a heart-to-heart talk. Take a look at Jesus' prayer times with his Father. I believe you can use the same types of key times to encourage your son toward more communication with you. And once communication with you is routinely established, it is a short transition to encourage your son to talk with God about the same things. Jesus drew aside and talked with his Father about five key topics. Make yourself available, and perhaps your son will talk with you about the same things.

1. *Jesus talked with his Father when things were going well.* After Jesus performed two amazing miracles—feeding the five thousand (Matthew 14:13-23) and healing a leper (Luke 5:12-16)—crowds of people were excited about him. If we had participated in something that extraordinary, we probably would have put out a press release and hired a publicist to get us an interview on one of the late-night talk shows. But not Jesus. At these times, when things were going incredibly well, he stole away and spent time alone with his Father.

People light up when allowed to talk about their successes, something in which they feel confident or of which they are proud. They will open up if they feel you are sincerely captivated by what they have to say. Your son's interests may not be your interests, but you can still show an interest and be proud of him. Your hobby might be working on small engines, while your son might be into chess and the debate team. Let him tell you about chess and debate. He may not know his way around a carburetor, but you may not be able to reason your way out of a cardboard box. Learn to appreciate the successes he reaches in the activities at which he excels. You could be raising a great statesman or attorney.

2. *Jesus talked with his Father when people wanted to crown him as king* (see John 6:15). How easy it would have been for Jesus to accept all the accolades people threw his way. Jesus' charisma drew people in, and they wanted to be connected with him, but he always deferred to his Father. He knew his Father could keep him grounded.

Your son's personality may cause people to be drawn to him. Even if he is somewhat of a loner, odds are he hangs out with other loners at least once in a while. His group of friends makes him feel wanted and accepted.

We all are born as relational beings, and our need for camaraderie is strong. That is why gangs pull so many young men into their clutches. Look for opportunities in which your son can talk to you about his buddies. Perhaps you will be able to discern his position in the group. For example, is he the leader, the strategist, the comedian, the risk taker, the lookout? Whatever his position, incorporate the strengths that placed him there in your relationship with him, and you will thereby enhance the closeness between the two of you.

Step Aside

Start a conversation with your son about things that are going well. Once he starts to talk, your job is simply to listen, nod, and smile. Let your chest well up. Let him see how proud his dad is of him.

3. *Jesus talked with his Father when he had a decision to make.* He actually spent all night in conversation with God before choosing his disciples (see Luke 6:12-13). Decision times offer obvious reasons to talk, so take full advantage when they roll around. The trick here is to learn to actually say less and

less. When your son is early elementary age, he will want to take your advice and listen to your sage wisdom. As he ages, the natural course of things is for him to make more and more of his own decisions, but your relationship can be such that he will still come to you to hear what you have to say.

Step Aside

Invite your son and his closest buddies to hang out with you and your buddies. Best case scenario: go on a weekend camping and hiking trip. Other ideas could include anything from bowling or basketball (old men vs. the kids) to yard work or cleaning out the garage.

4. *Jesus talked with his Father when his true identity was revealed.* In Luke 9:28-36, we read of a time when Jesus was amazingly transformed from his normal, daily appearance to his heavenly, glorified visage. Just before this happened, he was talking with his Father who was actually the one responsible for that awesome moment.

Realize your responsibility as a dad to provide everything necessary so your son can shine. Our son Matthew voiced his dreams, and his dad listened. Besides providing that movie camera I mentioned earlier, my husband also enrolled him in a college screenwriting program he wanted to attend. Those two investments acted as the catalyst for Matthew's burgeoning filmmaking career. He is fulfilling God's purpose for him as a result of God's blessing, Matthew's own drive, and his father's foresight to provide for him those early needs that became stepping-stones.

Step Aside

Try speaking in very casual tones when asking about or discussing with your son upcoming decisions. Comment in an almost off-handed manner. Resist the urge to tell him what to do, but if you're just dying to offer a few alternative suggestions, preface your words with, "You may want to think about..." or "Have you considered...?" Once into the conversation, write down the choices and list the probable positive and negative outcomes.

5. *Jesus talked to his Father when facing emotionally hard times.* In Matthew 26:36-38, Jesus knew he'd be facing the toughest time imaginable, his arrest and crucifixion, and he asked his friends to accompany him to Gethsemane. Jesus even told them, "My soul is overwhelmed with sorrow to the point of death. Stay here and keep watch with me."

Like Jesus, your son will need someone to talk to and to be with when he faces emotionally tough times. Realize that a small boy's loss of a prized toy, an elementary-aged boy's realization that he wasn't invited to a classmate's birthday party, or a high schooler's disappointment at being cut from the team all hold equal importance in the mind of that child at that point in time. Never belittle your son's honest frustrations.

Cultivate an atmosphere in which your son feels safe opening up emotionally to you about his disappointments and failures. Comments like "Man up" are not always appropriate. You can validate your son's hurt without sanctioning a victim mentality in him. If you close your door to him when he feels he needs you most, you may have a very hard time ever cracking it open again. In order for your son to grow up to be like Christ, preserve and mirror in your home the open relationship Jesus had with his Father.

Yes, if your son is going to be like Christ, a young man in his image, he will need to cultivate Jesus' habit #1 and sustain a strong relationship with God through his prayer life. This will be modeled in his strong relationship with his earthly father or some other male figure who fulfills that role in his life. Man-to-earthly-man communication can then easily be transitioned into a strong prayer life between him and God. Letting

Step Aside

Listen to your son's dreams. Guide him into an understanding of his responsibility to work toward his own dream and invest in his own vision. Provide the environment and as many of the means as you are able for your son to realize his true identity, gifts, and calling.

your son see and hear you pray for him will also motivate him to build his own prayer life with God.

Habit #2: Jesus proclaimed his relationship with his Father by preaching his Father's word. Jesus amazed people whenever he opened his month to teach his Father's truth. Why? Because "he taught them as one who had authority" (see Mark 1:21-22). The words that came from Jesus' mouth were never random. What comes out of the mouth reflects who a person really is. Think about it: John 1:14 identifies Jesus as "the Word [who] became flesh and made his dwelling among us." No wonder those who heard him

Step Aside

The next time your son looks a little down or approaches you with a problem, make a determined effort to listen. Before you make suggestions, express your opinion, or offer advice, stop. Take a few slow breaths, and then repeat to him the essence of what he just shared with you. This will show both of you that you really listened to what he had to say. Next, either say a silent prayer or have your son join you in prayer over the situation. Finally, encourage your son to work through the problem by guiding him as he talks through the handling of the situation. You do this by asking him leading questions aimed at helping him find the best solution for himself. Ask questions such as:

■ Where do you think your strong feelings are really coming from?

■ Why is this situation bothering you so much?

■ What practical things can you do to change the situation?

■ What do you lose by making that change?

■ What do you gain by making that change?

■ Are the gains worth it?

■ Can you think of any Scripture passages that would relate to this situation? If so, let's look them up and see how God expects you to apply his Word to this problem.

were amazed at his teaching. Jesus was literally God's Word speaking—the words from the pages of the Torah animated right before their eyes. Even so, Jesus always gave God the glory by proclaiming God's Word. This acknowledgment was borne out of a strong relationship with his Father.

Jesus had to know and trust his Father's Word in order to proclaim it. Several Scripture verses verify the fact that Jesus knew his Father's Word. For example, he taught and preached it in synagogues throughout Galilee (Matthew 4:23), and he used it to prove who he was (Luke 4:16-21).

Our sons will grow up into the image of Christ not only by knowing God's Word, but by proclaiming it. Knowing God's Word comes from reading it regularly. Proclaiming God's Word takes courage and practice. The best practice for this is for your son to know his own father's word and proclaim it.

It is said that imitation is the sincerest form of flattery. Nothing is more gratifying than to hear your children communicating a serious belief to another person and to realize that your child's fervor is about something you have taught him. Our youngest son, Mark, has watched his dad's financial success and has taken on his attitude toward credit. He is not as frugal with his cash yet, but because of what he has learned from his dad, he respects credit, he has not abused his emergency credit card, and he has not rushed to open his own accounts for fear of accruing bills he cannot pay. He readily shares the principles about credit that he learned from his father with his friends.

Sons want a father whose word they can trust. It is easier for our sons to trust God's Word when they have grown up in the habit of trusting their father's word.

The Bible holds the answers to all of the complexities life will throw at your son. Psalm 119 is the longest psalm in the Bible, and its main theme is the Word of God. Verses that will help your son include:

■ How can a young man keep his way pure? By living according to your word (v. 9).

■ Your word is a lamp to my feet and a light for my path (v. 105).

■ Direct my footsteps according to your word; let no sin rule over me (v. 133).

■ All your words are true; all your righteous laws are eternal (v. 160).

Read the Bible for yourself before your son is born, to him while he is small, and with him as he matures. For a time, I read Proverbs with my sons each night before they went to sleep. We would read a few verses until something popped out at us for discussion, and they would end their day talking with me and pondering over the wisdom taught in that book. Build wisdom by reading Proverbs, encourage worship by reading the Psalms, and help them get to know Jesus better by reading the Gospels.

There is something magnificent to be gleaned from every book in the Bible. Start early in your son's life and take your time. You have every night of his young life, and he is a captive audience. Soon your son will begin to repeat in his own words and from his own heart that which he trusts as truth from his heavenly Father.

Again, my son Mark showed me an example of this. While at college, he got a job walking the precincts during election time. There he was—an African American male approaching strangers' homes in the South. I must admit, I

Step Aside

Once your son can read on his own, assign a certain amount of Bible reading per night or week. He doesn't have to read an entire chapter at one sitting. He can read a few verses at a time, stopping whenever a point or observation needs to be made.

Make a plan now for the next two months. What book of the Bible are you going to read to/with your son? Decide on a definite starting date.

wasn't all that comfortable with that idea, and I communicated to him my concerns. His response was, "Mom, God is protecting me." Mark was living in Christ's image by repeating God's Word to me. He was proclaiming his relationship with his Father by preaching his Father's Word.

Habit #3: Jesus maintained his relationship with his Father through obedience by carrying out God's will. When a son is in relationship with a father who balances delight with discipline, the resultant harmony and joy emanating from that relationship is almost palpable.

It seems as though the great golfer Tiger Woods had that kind of relationship with his father. The world looked on as Tiger grew into the world-class golfer he is today under the watchful eye and guiding

Step Aside

Help your son build Jesus' third habit of obedience through the directed use of his time, his talent, and his treasure toward the things of God. Among other activities you could do, try the following.

Directed use of time:
1. Spend five minutes at bedtime reading verses from Proverbs.
2. Attend church every Sunday.

Directed use of talent:
1. Volunteer for three months to use your musical, art, or acting talent with the Sunday school at your church.
2. Volunteer your administrative skills to help out in the office of your local church, Christian school, or church-sponsored senior citizens' home.

Directed use of treasure: (I will talk extensively about this in chapter 10)
1. Tithe
2. For one day a month, skip lunch and use your lunch money for someone in need.

hand of his proud and loving father. Now that his father has passed away, Tiger hardly ever gives an interview in which he does not mention the enormously positive influence his father had on his life. The educational community center Tiger built is not only in his father's memory, but was actually his father's dream. This is a perfect modern-day example of a son carrying out the will of his father.

Immediately following the scriptural admonishment to children to obey their parents is the commandment to fathers concerning how they should raise their sons: "Fathers, do not exasperate your children; instead, bring them up in the training and instruction of the Lord" (Ephesians 6:4). You will raise a son who reflects the image of the Savior as you deal with him in a balanced manner. Your son will be inclined to obey your word and carry out your will. Then he will grow to be like Christ as he transfers that habit into his spiritual relationship. He will be inclined to obey God's Word and carry out God's will. As God's Word permeates every aspect of your life and practice, it will begin to do the same for your son.

NOTES

1. "Habit," http://dictionary.reference.com/browse/habit.

2. "Habits," http://www.quoteworld.org/categories/habits.

3. "Single Parent Statistics," http://singleparents.about.com/od/legalissues/p/portrait.htm.

4. Glenn Sacks, "Are Boys Better Off without Fathers?" *San Francisco Chronicle*, August 31, 2005.

5. Source: U.S. Census Bureau, Current Population Survey, Annual Social and Economic Supplement, 2004, Racial Statistics Branch, Populations Division, http://www.census.gov/population/socdemo/race/black/ppl-186/tab4.pdf, accessed November 5, 2008.

6. Linda Malone-Colon and Alex Roberts, "Marriage and the Well-Being of African American Boys," Center for Marriage and Families at the Institute for American Values, Research Brief no. 2, Future of the Black Family Series, November 2006, http://center.americanvalues.org.

7. Gillis Triplett, "What Every African American Must Learn about Raising Boys," http://www.gillistriplett.com/manhood/articles/raising_boys.html.

8. Ibid.

6
The Leader in Ministry

According to the Internet definition on About.com, "A simple definition of leadership is that leadership is the art of motivating a group of people to act towards achieving a common goal. Put even more simply, the leader is the inspiration and director of the action. He or she is the person in the group who possesses the combination of personality and skills that makes others want to follow his or her direction. In business, leadership is welded to performance. Effective leaders are those who increase their company's bottom lines." In other words, a leader does not have to be a president, pastor, or CEO. Every person can cultivate leadership qualities, and this chapter will discuss becoming like Jesus in the area of leadership.[1]

Talk about a purpose-driven life: Jesus was very clear about his own purpose, and he has never been deterred from it. He told his disciples that his very sustenance was to obey his father. "My food," said Jesus, "is to do the will of him who sent me and to finish his work" (John 4:34). And Jesus' work was clearly defined to his parents before his birth. The angel Gabriel gave Mary this message: "He will be great and will be called the Son of the Most High. The Lord God will give him the throne of his father David, and he will reign over the house of Jacob forever; his kingdom will never end" (Luke 1:32-33). An even more specific purpose statement was given to Joseph when he found out about Mary's pregnancy. Matthew 1:21 says, "She [Mary] will give birth to a son, and you are to give him the name Jesus, because he will save his people from their sins." Jesus was a child born to fulfill a great destiny, to be a great leader. We are never given any hint as to whether Joseph and Mary ever felt apprehension or discussed misgivings about their abilities to parent this kind of kid, but I would be willing to bet that the subject came up now and then. It looks as though they did a pretty good job, because Jesus did indeed work to fulfill his destiny. This chapter will look at some of the characteristics of Jesus as a ministry leader and suggest some ways to parent your son toward the great destiny as a leader God has planned for him.

Integrity

Jesus was definitely a man of integrity when it came to leading in his ministry. He repeatedly told his followers who he was and acted in accordance with what he told them. Wikipedia defines *integrity* as "the basing of one's actions on an internally consistent framework of principles. . . . One is said to have integrity to the extent that everything he does and believes is based on the same core set of values."[2] And that describes Jesus' behavior. Here are a few examples:

- "Then Jesus declared, 'I am the bread of life. He who comes to me will never go hungry, and he who believes in me will never be thirsty'" (John 6:35). Jesus was saying, "I'll fill you with everything you need."
- "When Jesus spoke again to the people, he said, 'I am the light of the world. Whoever follows me will never walk in darkness, but will have the light of life'" (John 8:12). Jesus was saying, "I'll direct you to exactly where you should go."
- "I told you that you would die in your sins; if you do not believe that I am the one I claim to be, you will indeed die in your sins" (John 8:24). Jesus communicated clearly the consequences of failing to do what had to be done.

■ "I am the good shepherd. The good shepherd lays down his life for the sheep" (John 10:11). Jesus sacrificed himself for his followers.

■ "What about the one whom the Father set apart as his very own and sent into the world? Why then do you accuse me of blasphemy because I said, 'I am God's Son'? Do not believe me unless I do what my Father does" (John 10:36-37). Jesus knew the importance of being accountable to someone himself. He needed a "mentor."

■ "Jesus said to [Martha], 'I am the resurrection and the life. He who believes in me will live, even though he dies'" (John 11:25). Jesus proved that he indeed was the resurrection by bringing Lazarus back to life.

■ "Jesus answered, 'I am the way and the truth and the life. No one comes to the Father except through me'" (John 14:6). Jesus was responsible for the welfare of his followers.

■ "Believe me when I say that I am in the Father and the Father is in me; or at least believe on the evidence of the miracles themselves" (John 14:11). Jesus lived as the example to his followers of how they should live.

A leader is nothing without integrity. A leader must be who he says he is and do what he says he will do.

Step Aside

Take another look at the verses mentioned above. When encouraging your son to be a leader with integrity, compare those verses with these qualities culled from Jesus' leadership example. Talk him through the qualities below that relate to his particular leadership challenge.

■ A leader fulfills his followers' needs.

■ A leader directs. He knows what his followers should do. He knows how they should do it and expects them to do it.

■ A leader clearly communicates consequences.

■ A leader is the first person to know all the ins and outs of the business.

■ A leader is accountable to someone higher than himself.

■ A leader accepts the fact that he is responsible for the welfare of his followers.

■ A leader lives as an example to those being led.

The soul is the spiritual part of a person that shines through in his words and actions. If your son's soul is healthy, his words and actions will bear that out. And the ultimate proof of a healthy soul is when a person's words and actions line up perfectly with God's intentions. This is what we see when we observe a person operating in his purpose; or in other words, when a person operates in his ministry. This is integrity.

We can see four cornerstones of leadership demonstrated in Jesus' life. To help us remember those four cornerstones, we will use an acronym: the CODE to integrity is *consistency, organization, diligence,* and *ethics.*

Integrity Shown through Consistency

A person of integrity is consistent. Wordnet defines *integrity* as "an undivided or unbroken completeness or totality with nothing wanting."[3] Consistency shows itself in a person who is dependable, reliable, and responsible. That person's loyalty is undivided and complete. This describes Jesus to a T. We can depend on him. He's reliable. As difficult as it was, he carried out his responsibility. His loyalty to God and to his followers was undivided and complete.

Under the above definition, consistency not only manifests itself in what a person does, but in how he does it. Projects are completed punctually and perfectly. Everything Jesus did happened at the exact right time, under the exact right conditions, in the exact right way.

I found another definition from a technology site on the Internet that more directly shows that consistency is a quality of integrity. BBN Technologies' Web glossary defines *consistency* as "the value judgment that a transmission, message, or document has not been modified accidentally or maliciously since it was authored."[4] Do you see that? *Integrity* means the message has not been modified since it was authored.

Hebrews 13:8 says that "Jesus Christ is the same yesterday and today and forever." As God come in the flesh, Jesus didn't ever change; his words and his actions always carried the same message.

He told his followers to love their neighbors, and they saw him have compassion on people. He told the disciples to serve one another, and he washed their feet.

If your son will be like Christ, he will have to live out his integrity by developing the attribute of consistency. Help him with this by holding his

Step Aside

Any responsibility can be used as a teaching moment for instilling the principle of integrity through consistency. For what is your son responsible? Is he consistent in carrying out his responsibilities? He will never learn responsibility without being given responsibility. At every age, he should be responsible for something.

List some things for which your son is responsible. Let this list be his report card. Grade him on how consistent he is in dealing with his responsibilities.

Responds politely to adults.   _____
Completes homework without
   being told to do so.   _____
Is ready for school on time.   _____

_____.   _____

_____.   _____

_____.   _____

_____.   _____

_____.   _____

_____.   _____

_____.   _____

_____.   _____

_____.   _____

feet to the fire when it comes to expectations. Teach him to be who he says he is. If he says he is a friend, encourage him to be there when his friends need him, even if that happens to be at a time that conflicts with the party he wants to attend. Insist that he follow through with the promises he makes, even if time has passed and he doesn't feel like doing whatever it was anymore. Hold him accountable for the choices he makes.

We required that our boys serve in some capacity in our church. While Matthew served as president of the youth group, Mark chose to work on the usher board. Great. He already owned the uniform: a long-sleeved white shirt, black pants, and a black tie. The first few weeks were fabulous. Everyone made a big fuss about Mark standing at his post and doing his job. However, after the excitement wore off, there were meetings to attend, and the monotony of the routine and same outfit week after week quickly set in. He decided to quit. Oh no. We would not allow it. He had made a commitment. We agreed that he would serve for a specified amount of time before he could choose another auxiliary.

You can start to teach the integrity of consistency early in your son's life. With little boys, for example, expect them to be polite. Nothing irks me more than a little child who is allowed to be rude. Social civility is necessary in business and in our general contact with others. Be firm in requiring your young son to say hello or to politely acknowledge an adult who enters a room.

Integrity Shown through Organization

A person of integrity is organized. While the biblical record does not provide us with much detail about Jesus' administrative style, neither does it ever reveal him as being confused, losing track of his disciples or his ministry goals, or missing an important appointment. Rather, he seemed to be systematic about doing things "decently and in order" as Paul later advised (1 Corinthians 14:40).

Jesus sought John's baptism because it was proper (Matthew 3:13-15). He emerged from the wilderness, ready to begin his ministry—with a routine that was consistent as he traveled from town to town, visiting the synagogues, preaching the gospel of repentance, and healing the sick (Matthew 4:23). He systematically recruited twelve disciples, students whom he would train and to whom he would ultimately delegate the work of ministry. And when the time came, Jesus resolutely turned his face to Jerusalem to face what awaited him there. He had a vision, and he had a plan for fulfilling that vision—and a multitude of prophecies along the way. He had to have been organized to get everything done that God had set before him!

Your son's integrity will shine when he leads an organized lifestyle that allows him to get everything done. When he makes a promise or a commitment, he will be able to stick to it because he is organized enough not to let other things get in the way.

I am always impressed with my senior high school student athletes who achieve a place on the honor roll. They tell me they want to go to college, and they have big dreams about successful careers outside of their sport. As much as they love to compete, keeping their grades high throughout the sports season says a lot about their integrity. One particular athlete comes to mind who exemplified this. T.J. (Tyrod) Anderson was an honor roll student since his very first progress report as a freshman. I watched him for all four years as he competed vigorously in sports, enthusiastically participated in other school activities, and kept his grades high. It wasn't always easy, and he has told me about late nights he spent reading and at his com-puter to get everything done. During his junior and senior years, the football team garnered the league championship, so you know that took an enormous amount of practice and travel time. Still T.J. has emerged victorious, not only on the field, but in his academics, and he will graduate as our school's valedictorian.

To accomplish all that he has to do, T.J. has to be extremely well organized. He schedules his homework and practice times. During early morning hours in the off-season, I have seen him working out on the field and in the weight room. And I didn't mention yet that he also works a part-time job. I can count on T.J. not only to have his assignments ready, but to have been attentive to the assignments so he can conduct intelligent classroom discussions about the topics at hand. This is a young man whose organizational skills keep him consistent, which allows him to follow through with work given, promises and commitments made, and appointments scheduled. T.J. is a young man of integrity.

If your son has problems maintaining consistency in any area, it could be because he is lacking some basic organizational skills. If he is unorganized, he will probably forget to do something, and this will cause him anxiety, poor grades, or missed opportunities. Sometimes responsibilities build up gradually, and before you know it, he is swamped with tons of things that must be accomplished. Our sons can be involved in so many different activities that a boy with poor organizational skills can quickly become frustrated. Scale back. List and then prioritize his involvements. Every boy is not the same, so be realistic about how many hours there are in a day and how

Step Aside

To help your son organize his life, do the following:

■ Write out a list of all the things in which he is involved (school, church, sports, community service, scouting, etc.). Make two copies of this list. He uses one; you use the other.
■ Assign a time value to each activity (e.g., scouting takes three hours per week).
■ Categorize the items on the list as essential or nonessential.
■ Prioritize the items on the essential list from most to least urgent.
■ Prioritize the items on the nonessential list from most to least favorable.
■ Compare your list with your son's list.
■ Discuss the differences.
■ Agree on an essential list.
■ Discuss how nonessentials can either fit into his schedule or be put on hold until necessary time is freed up.
■ Draft a schedule that he can live with, one on which he can check things off when projects or activities are accomplished, so that he can visibly see the progress he is making.

many things your son, with his unique set of gifts and challenges, can actually handle. Depending on your son's age, you can do this together or you can let him do it while you act as an adviser giving your input to and approval of the final list.

Integrity Shown through Diligence

A person of integrity is diligent. Diligence goes a step beyond consistence. When you are consistent, you keep doing a certain thing; but when you add diligence to the equation, you are pursuing your goal with persevering attention in a painstaking way. In other words, it matters not only that you finish, but that you finish well.

Jesus finished well what he started. His mission was a difficult one, and we see his very human side when, in the Garden of Gethsemane, he questioned God, asking if there was any other way to save us other than passing through the terrible death by crucifixion (see Matthew 26:39, 42). Nevertheless, Jesus lived the perfect life he had to live for us. Hebrews 4:15 says, "For we do not have a high priest who is unable to sympathize with our weaknesses, but we have one who has been tempted in every-way, just as we are—yet was without sin." And Hebrews 12:2 says, "Let us fix our eyes on Jesus, the author and perfecter of our faith, who for the joy set before him endured the

Step Aside

Diligence reveals itself through a mind-set tuned to excellence. Does your son strive for excellence, or is he content with the status quo? Jot down some ways in which you can help your son develop the attribute of diligence. Here are some ideas to get you started:

■ Refuse to turn in class assignments with mistakes scratched out.

■ Add something extra to a school project (e.g., instead of doing just the required poster, make the poster three-dimensional).

■ Mow the lawn and trim the hedges.

cross, scorning its shame, and sat down at the right hand of the throne of God." Jesus finished perfectly what he came to do.

I find it quite disheartening when the majority of my high school students do just enough to get by. They ask, "What's the least number of pages you will accept for this composition?" or "What's the shortest book on the novel list?" or "Which is the easiest project I can choose?" Even though they request light duty, they want high grades. What ever happened to pride in workmanship and giving something one's all?

Perhaps our sons see lazy tendencies in the adults in their lives. How quick are we to say, "That's not in my contract," or "Why should I extend myself?" Perhaps they see us looking for every possible quick fix, even in the little things: get in shape in ten minutes a day, get in touch with God in short prayer bursts, and get close to our loved ones through instant messaging.

Diligence is not a sprint. By definition, diligence involves persevering, and perseverance is a function of a timeline. Doing things well takes time. If your son will be like Christ, he will do well to slow down and take his time getting things done in an excellent manner.

Integrity Shown through Ethics

A person of integrity is ethical. According to Webster's Third New International Dictionary, *integrity* is "adherence to a code of values; utter sincerity, honesty, candor; completeness." We call a code of values, ethics. Ethics is the philosophy of analyzing right and wrong. Although everyone doesn't live by the same code, everyone has an ethical or moral code.

Strictly by definition, then, one could make the argument that criminals are ethical individuals because they live by a moral code. Lying is considered a good thing if it keeps one out of trouble. Robbery is okay if the owner didn't deserve to have whatever it was anyway. He who has the money and the power makes the rules. "Do unto others before they do unto you," is a smart policy. And no matter what, they won't snitch on their partners in crime, even if those partners are guilty of committing a horrendous act.

At first glance, you may see the above statements as obviously reprehensible, but a closer evaluation will expose these thoughts as statements of values held, not only by criminals and participants in gang culture, but by society at large. Just consider how prominent government leaders are caught in lies, and various laws and policies favor the powerful and neglect the already marginalized.

A truly ethical code must be based on that which is intrinsically right and true. For an ethical code to mean anything at all, there must be an ultimate standard of truth from which morals flow. As Christians, we base our conception of right and wrong on the tenets found in the Bible. God is the author of absolute truth, and the only correct and just moral code flows from his Word. Jesus lived by that code. If our sons are going to be like him and be young men of integrity, they must internalize and live by that same ethical code as well.

Step Aside

What does your son believe is right and wrong? What is his code of ethics? Start a discussion by asking him if he agrees with the following statements. You may be surprised by what he says.

- Lying is a good thing if it keeps you out of trouble.
- Robbery is okay if the owner didn't deserve to have whatever it was anyway.
- He who has the money and the power makes the rules.
- Do unto others before they do unto you.
- No matter what, don't snitch on your partners even if those partners are guilty of committing a horrendous act.

NOTES

1. About.com., http://sbinfocanada.about.com/od/leadership/g/leadership.htm.

2. "Integrity," http://en.wikipedia.org/wiki/Integrity

3. "Integrity," http://wordnet.princeton.edu/perl/webwn.

4. "Integrity," http://BBN Technologies, www.bbn.com/glossary/I.

7
The Master Choosing His Disciples

Jesus was 100 percent God and 100 percent man. As man, he interacted with other men and women, even considering some of them his friends. In this chapter, we are going to explore the idea of friendship, wrapping up by looking at how Jesus handled it and grasping some truths we can pass on to our sons.

My children are comfortable in social settings because they have always been around groups of people. Even though I was a stay-at-home mom until my boys were school-age, they interacted all the time with family members and the children in Sunday school. They also fellowshipped with children their age at my monthly Mommy and Me meeting.

Our responsibility to teach our children the value of friendship can begin at a very early stage. Nothing valuable is built into our sons overnight. We want our sons to choose good friends and be good friends when they get older, so it makes sense to start training them in this art early. We don't know anything from Scripture about Jesus' childhood friends, but I believe his parents taught him social skills early. After all, by the age of twelve, he was comfortable with and able to speak intelligently to the synagogue leaders.

By modeling friendly behavior before them with our own friends and allowing them opportunities to engage in social activities with other children, our preschool-age sons will begin to reach out and make new friends of their own. Our observation of their playtime will afford us opportunities to comment on such values as sharing and playing together nicely. We can also help them to respond properly to behaviors that are less than welcome—such as verbal or physical acts of aggression. Go further than just stopping unwanted behavior. Gently teach why that behavior is unfavorable and help the child to understand what the proper response or behavior should be.

I remember the first birthday party of a child I did not know, to which my son Mark was invited when he was only three. I accompanied Mark to the party and watched as the children played comfortably together. Here were youngsters I didn't know interacting with my three-year-old son and he with them just as effortlessly as if they had known each other for twenty years. I think that was the first time I realized my sons would have lives separate from mine one day and I had better start preparing them for it. After all, everyone with older kids kept telling me how quickly those toddler years would pass. (Now that my sons are adults, I see how right those other parents were!)

When your son enters preschool or kindergarten, you won't be around all the time to make an on-the-spot analysis of each situation. However, the type of teaching you have been able to give because of your personal observations will enable him to begin to discern the type of people with whom he can form healthy relationships when you are not around.

When my friend Linda's son Shawn was in the sixth grade, God chose to offer him an opportunity to be a good friend. At an age when everyone wants to fit in, Shawn decided to be different. A new student, Dean, arrived after school had begun for the year; he was deaf and went to every class with an interpreter. Most of the kids stared at Dean and whispered when he walked by, but Shawn took a different approach. He checked a book out of the library on sign language and started teaching himself.

All of this was happening under Linda's radar. As a matter of fact, it wasn't until she went to a school program and witnessed Shawn signing that she knew what he had done. When she asked him what prompted him to learn sign language and why he didn't tell her about it, he said simply, "It was the right thing to do, Mom. No one should be alone. Besides," he shared with a grin, "I can talk anytime now and not get in trouble."

Shawn never explained why he didn't tell his mom, and she did not push him. Over the next year, Shawn and Dean became good friends. Their friendship affected many of the students in the school in a positive way, and Dean became a very popular guy—not that Shawn's stepping in would be labeled the reason, but Linda believes it was certainly a catalyst. Dean moved away a few years later, and to this day Shawn always takes a different road whenever it's the right thing to do.

A word of caution here against prejudice, parents. The type of people you would pick as friends may not be the type of people your boys pick. Be sure that the guidelines you set are biblically based, making them spiritually sound. For example, ethnicity should not be a boundary to friendship, but bad character should be. Social status should not be a boundary to friendship, but a dangerous lifestyle should be. Appearance or a physical disability should not be a boundary to friendship, but involvement in questionable activities should be. Friendship is valuable, and good friends are priceless.

Know Thyself

Eleanor Roosevelt said, "Friendship with oneself is all-important because without it one cannot be friends with anyone else in the world." Being friends with oneself implies knowing oneself, so it is important for us to rear our sons so

Step Aside

The next time you take your preschooler to the park or to a play group, observe closely how he interacts with other children. Note whether he is the aggressor, the compliant follower, the observer, etc. You will be looking at your son's natural temperament playing itself out. Resist the urge to change it; embrace the urge to direct and enhance it.

that they know and are comfortable with who they are. We are to study our sons and discover how God has bent them so we can then fall in line with God and direct them toward fulfilling their purpose. This starts with their name. Since we cannot observe our children before they are born, I believe we can ask for God's guidance in giving them a name that will be in agreement with his will for them.

The name Jesus means "Savior," thus carrying the significance of who he is. As we learned earlier, the angel told Joseph "You are to give him the name Jesus, because he will save his people from their sins" (Matthew 1:21). Jesus is also known as Immanuel, which means "God with us" (Matthew 1:23). So every time we say Jesus' name, we are calling upon his attributes and declaring that we recognize who he is.

Likewise, our sons' names are important. Think about this: every time you call out to your son, you are not only calling him by his name, you are calling him by the meaning of that name. Be very careful not to choose a name that just sounds good.

I did some study on the temperaments when I was pregnant with Matthew, and I was very concerned about what to name him. I depended on God to lead me to the name that would correspond with his temperament. I settled on the name Matthew because it means "gift of God." Truly, my oldest son is that gift, not only to me, but to others around him. From early in life, he has been sensitive to spiritual things and has exhibited the gift of discernment. He is zealous for his faith, and throughout his life, he has not been ashamed of being a Christian and wanting all his friends to know his Savior. You see, every time anyone calls my son's name, they are actually prefacing their comments with its meaning. Literally, they are saying, "Gift of God, how are you today?" "Gift of God, can you give me the answer to that question?" "Gift of God, I'd like to talk to you." How's that for building self-esteem?

I followed the same reasoning with the naming of my second son. Mark means "mighty warrior," and that he is. Mark is an athlete par excellence. All he has to do is observe a sport and he can perform it. He can hit a baseball, throw and catch a football, and dribble and shoot a basketball. It took him no time at all as a child to learn how to swim and dive. Spiritually speaking, Mark has a heart for the Lord and is growing to be a warrior for him.

Be attentive to and careful of what you name your son. Starting with his name, you can begin to teach him who he is in temperament and in Christ. He will live up to what he believes about himself.[1]

Know Thy Friends

Once your son knows himself, he is better prepared to make judgments as to the kinds of people he needs to have around him. Consider these quotes on friendship:

> "Tell me what company thou keepest, and I'll tell thee what thou art."
>
> —Miguel de Cervantes,
> sixteenth-century Spanish novelist

> "True happiness consists not in the multitude of friends, but in their worth and choice."
>
> —Samuel Johnston,
> eighteenth-century British lexicographer

> "Associate yourself with men of good quality if you esteem your own reputation; for 'tis better to be alone than in bad company."
>
> —George Washington

Although Jesus was constantly thronged by crowds, he surrounded himself with just a few carefully handpicked individuals with whom he shared the intimate secrets and moments of his life. Throughout the Gospels, we find Jesus taking aside his select group to explain things in detail to them alone. So who were these guys? They were purposely chosen and temperamentally different.

Purposely Chosen Mark 3:13-19 relates to Jesus' appointment of the special Twelve.

> Jesus went up on a mountainside and called to him those he wanted, and they came to him. He appointed twelve—designating them apostles—that they might be with him and that he might send them out to preach and to have authority to drive out demons. These are the twelve he appointed: Simon (to whom he gave the name Peter); James son of Zebedee and his brother John (to them he gave the name Boanerges, which means Sons of Thunder); Andrew, Philip, Bartholomew, Matthew, Thomas, James son of Alphaeus, Thaddaeus, Simon the Zealot and Judas Iscariot, who betrayed him.

Jesus did not haphazardly choose these men. He called out each one specifically and extended an invitation to follow him. And once those called accepted the invitation, as shown in the above passage, Jesus then formally ordained them for the work they had to do.

In the same way, direct your son to be purposeful about the friends he invites into his life. Point out the wisdom of surrounding himself with guys who have something going for themselves. He is a star with a bright future, so it only makes sense to hitch his wagon to other stars, other young men with purpose and direction. If guys have nothing better to do than hang out on the corner or sit on the porch all day, how are they benefiting his life? These are the types of friends that end up with their empty hands out, expecting your son, their "ace buddy road dawg," to fill them while they sit and brag about whom they know rather than what they have done.

Matthew has caught this vision and impresses me with the young men he knows and calls his friends. Two of his friends, Bing and Nate, come to mind. While serving our high school as our American Legion Boys' State representative, Matthew met Bing Chen. During a weeklong conference on government, a mock election was held and Bing's peers elected him governor. Bing's and Matthew's paths crossed again while working for Disney one summer while they were in college. Bing was still involved in politics via student government at the University of Pennsylvania. Nate Mitchell is no less notable. He and Matthew met while they were both students at Biola University, and Nate is running for representative of the 60th Congressional District of California. How cool is that to have a potential congressman for a good friend!

Temperamentally Different In addition to choosing guys who had something going for themselves, Jesus chose men with a variety of characteristics. He seems to have chosen at least one guy exhibiting the traits of each of the four temperaments I studied while raising my children—the sanguine, the choleric, the melancholy, and the phlegmatic. In brief, the child with the sanguine personality is the entertainer, the choleric is the controller, the melancholy is the perfectionist, and the phlegmatic is the peacemaker. What's the wisdom of having friends of different temperaments? Simple—your son has strengths and weaknesses; if he is surrounded by friends exactly like him, his strengths may be built, but his weaknesses will also be magnified. By surrounding himself with guys of different personality types, his strengths and weaknesses will be brought into balance—and so will those of his friends.

Peter reminds me most of the sanguine personality because he is such a talker. He was constantly putting his foot in his mouth. Sometimes he was right; sometimes he was wrong. One popular Bible teacher says Jesus probably spent an awful lot of time shaking his head and rolling his eyes toward heaven, sighing, "Peter, Peter, Peter."

The great thing about having a sanguine as a friend is that life will never be boring. Sanguines are on the go; they love to laugh

> **Step Aside**
>
> Ask your teenage son if he knows his friends' future plans. Let this be the beginning of a discussion about the wisdom of choosing friends who have something going for themselves.

and have a good time. They are the life of the party; however, sanguines need to be tempered by the other personality styles, because left to themselves, they will never get anything done. They'll throw the party, but they won't clean up afterward.

James and John, referred to in scripture as the "sons of thunder," remind me of the choleric personality. Perhaps they were given that name because they had loud, commanding voices, were thundering preachers, or were zealous in their service to God. Nevertheless, we know from John's gospel and epistles that he was full of love and tenderness.

Both James and John were leaders. Every friendship group needs sharp guys like them who can visualize and execute plans. They can be the catalyst that keeps themselves and everybody else inspired and moving forward. Be aware, though, that some cholerics can lead in a negative direction. Gang leaders, tyrants, and dictators exhibit choleric traits.

Thomas could possibly have been the melancholy one of the bunch. He was the thinker. There would be no pulling the wool over this guy's eyes. The melancholy guy thinks things through, making lists that will help him logically make sense of what is going on. He will keep everybody grounded. Every friendship group needs the realistic person. Unfortunately, Thomas allowed the weakness of his personality to earn him the dubious distinction of being known as a doubter. He was overly cautious. For some reason, he wasn't with the other disciples when Jesus first appeared to them after his resurrection (see John 20:24-31). Perhaps Thomas's strict melancholy logic blocked his ability to accept the possibility of the miraculous.

The fourth personality style is the phlegmatic, and I see some of those traits in Andrew. Phelgmatics are followers and great diplomats and counselors. This guy's role in the friendship is to bring people together and keep the peace. John 1:35, 40 tells us that Andrew was one of John the Baptist's followers. When Andrew heard John proclaim Jesus to be the Lamb of God, he started following Jesus and shared the news with his brother, Simon Peter, no doubt in hopes of convincing him to follow Jesus too (see John 1:40-42). Every group needs a balancing peacemaker, but a group full of phlegmatics would be so fickle that they would have a hard time staying focused on one thing long enough for it to profit them in any substantial way.

All the temperaments in the friendship group need to keep a keen eye out for toxic acquaintances. Judas Iscariot was one. He allowed himself to be influenced by Satan and ended up betraying Jesus. Every friend your son selects is a freewill moral agent who can make both positive and negative choices. As you encourage your son to surround himself with guys of all the temperaments, remind him that everybody is not necessarily good for him. Some people are best left alone because their twisted thinking and poor choices can adversely affect the whole group. "Do not be misled: 'Bad company corrupts good character'" (1 Corinthians 15:33).

Cautiously Evaluated These days it's not enough to teach our sons the difference between a friend and a stranger. We must warn them about Internet predators as well, who sneak into their bedrooms via their computer screens and seek to lure them into danger and death.

So that we could keep a closer watch on our boys' online activities, they weren't allowed to have the Internet on the computer in their room. And they were only to chat online with people we knew. Still, as much as we warned them about Internet dangers, Matthew didn't get it. He began communicating with an unknown person via one of the popular online social networking sites. In his mind, once he had chatted back and forth a few times and received a picture, the person was no longer a stranger.

One day Matthew asked if he could attend the finals of a local track meet. This was a somewhat unusual request since he wasn't immediately involved in that level of the sport. Upon my further investigation, he revealed that he wanted to meet a friend at this meet, the girl whom he had been chatting with online. It actually took some convincing before he understood that anyone can post a picture on the Internet, and he really knew nothing at all about this person. This "young lady" could just as easily have been a six feet seven ex-wrestler and ex-con with a penchant for unsavory activities with teenage boys. One shove into an unmarked van, and we never would have seen Matthew again. Matthew finally understood my point and cut off all communication with the unknown person.

Step Aside

When your child is in preschool and kindergarten, you will probably be very active in selecting his friends. But once he is in early elementary school, he will begin to select his own friends. Open a dialogue with your son about his friends, using the following questions. You may have to reword some of the questions based on your son's age.

■ How do you select your friends?

■ Do you have any recognizable criteria for selecting your friends?

■ What do your really know about your friends?

■ Can you see the personality differences in your friends? Who is the sanguine, the choleric, the melancholy, and the phlegmatic in your group of friends?

■ Where is each friend going in life? Does each one have future plans?

Encourage your son to welcome friends into his life who are of noble character and of different personality types. Getting to know people who are not exactly like him will give your son an appreciation for and a love of the various types of people God has created. Your son will become a well-rounded individual and will develop a heart like God's.

NOTE

1. I highly recommend the book *Wired That Way* by Marita and Florence Littauer (Ventura: Regal Books, 2006). You can also purchase the companion workbook, which has an easy-to-use questionnaire to help assess personality types.

8

The Man in and under Authority

A wise son honors authority and knows the importance of obeying the law. However, like many of the other practices discussed in this book, your son will neither honor authority nor obey the law unless you do. As a high school teacher, I know exactly how contentious a parent-teacher conference will be even before I meet the parents. Students who treat school rules with disdain inevitably prove to be parented by folks who believe loopholes exist for their child and approach the school's rules as debatable rather than firm. I must employ inordinate tact and resolve in those meetings, because both parent and child enter challenging the authority of the school's rules.

Why are urban gangs attractive to so many young men? Why do young men in relationships turn violent and become abusive? What's up with all the school shootings? Why the epidemic of disobedience and disrespect toward authority figures, be they teachers, police officers, or even parents? I believe the crisis of violence, disrespect, and immorality in America is directly related to our disdain for authority yet our ultimate hunger for it. Without leadership, there is chaos; but without morality, there can be no positive leadership.

Humanity functions by the leader-follower model. Parents teach children how to function in the world, and then children grow up to be parents who teach their children the same lessons. Teachers teach students, bosses teach employees, drill sergeants teach privates, upper management teaches middle management—you get the picture. It follows then that if the followers are sick, the illness was spread to them by diseased leadership. This explains our current state of affairs in America: we no longer honor the tenets of the Bible as it lays out absolute truth for us, and our contempt for Christian principles has led us to push away the very thing that can rescue us—agreement with and acquiescence to godly authority.

How did Jesus relate to authority? Did he accept and obey it, or did he buck against it? After all, Jesus is God, so while he was on earth, wasn't everyone subject to his authority? The answers can be seen as we take a look at how Jesus related to the different types of authority he encountered: the authority of God, authorities established by God, and other authorities who wanted to be followed.

Authority Established by God

I spoke at length in chapter 5 about how Jesus lived his life on earth under the authority of his heavenly Father. Jesus said, "I have come down from heaven not to do my will but to do the will of him who sent me" (John 6:38).

Jesus also submitted to the earthly authorities God established. Romans 13:1 says, "Everyone must submit himself to the governing authorities, for there is no authority except that which God has established. The authorities that exist have been established by God." Jesus paid taxes (Mark 12:14-17), answered to the high priest (Matthew 26:62-64), and allowed himself to be arrested when the time was right (compare John 7:30 with Mark 14:48-49). Jesus even submitted to death (John 10:17-18). So you see, the pattern of obeying authority is clear in the life of Jesus.

To maintain order in our lives, God has established other authorities, such as parents, governments (this includes civic officials like police officers), spiritual leaders, and teachers. It is our responsibility to raise our sons in Christ's image, teaching them to respect and yield to all the authorities God has established.

Parents Parents, we are the first authority figures our children encounter. They are given a pretty strict injunction in Ephesians 6:1-3 regarding how they are to relate to us. "Children, obey your parents in the Lord, for this is right. 'Honor your father and mother' —which is the first commandment with a promise—'that it may go well with you and that you may enjoy long life on the earth.'" God is telling our children that their very life is directly dependent on their obedience to us. We parents are quick to harp on this verse when our kids decide to be rebellious. We feel justified musing, *Johnny had better cool it before he suffers some serious consequences from God for not listening to me.*

Hold your horses. Before tossing Scripture at children, let's be sure we have caught the context for ourselves. The passage says that kids are to obey their parents "in the Lord." Are we directing, disciplining, and discipling our sons under God's direction or in our own understanding? Are we living before them as a demonstration of the type of life they should live, or have we taken the ungodly stance that says, "Do as I say, not as I do"? Perhaps our sons don't honor us because we are not living honorably before them.

Ephesians 6:4, the very next verse of the above-mentioned passage, continues with an admonition specifically to fathers: "Fathers, do not exasperate your children; instead, bring them up in the training and instruction of the Lord." In other words, we parents are responsible before God for how we deal with our children. We are to raise them in a manner that not only makes God proud

> **Step Aside**
> Evaluate yourself. Are you living honorably before your children? How do you present yourself in public? Are your children proud to bring their friends home to meet you? Can they trust you to operate in all areas "in the Lord"?

of them, but that makes God pleased with us. Ultimately our kids are only on loan to us from God. What shape will they be in when we finish with them and return them to him?

While teaching middle school some years ago, I witnessed dishonorable parenting. I had been having some trouble getting one student to complete his assignments. Chauncey was a remarkable athlete and figured he didn't have to excel in academics; his prowess on the basketball court was going to propel him to stardom. Of course, I knew that thousands of young men thought the same thing. There weren't enough NBA teams to use them all, so Chauncey would need more than a great jump shot to guarantee his success in life. I figured joining forces with his mother could work to begin to convince him of the importance of his schoolwork.

When his mom showed up for our parent-teacher conference, I immediately saw at least one of the sources of Chauncey's rebellion. She was a stunning beauty, as statuesque as a runway model, and perfectly coifed and made up. The problem was her outfit. She unashamedly strolled onto the campus in four-inch black patent leather stilettos, a clingy, low-cut sweater, and a mini skirt so short that not much was left to the imagination. The teenage boys on campus unabashedly gawked at her.

Although this mom was oblivious to her son's feelings, Chauncey's embarrassment shadowed his face like a complete lunar eclipse. His failure to apply himself to academics was his way of showing his dishonor toward his mother. He was passively-aggressively saying, "You don't respect yourself, so I refuse to respect you. You're hurting me by embarrassing me in how you represent yourself, so I'm going to hurt you by embarrassing you over my low grades."

Governments (Kings, Presidents, Police) We have already read Romans 13:1, which says, "Let every person be subject to the governing authorities; for there is no authority except from God, and those authorities that exist have been instituted by God" (NRSV). Obeying the law is right and important. The laws of God and the laws of our land are in place to protect both our physical lives and our property. Laws regulate how members of a civilized society behave toward one another. Without laws, there would be utter chaos. Our sons exhibit Christlike character when they obey the law. The exception is when human laws contradict the laws of God; then we are subject to the higher law of the Lord.

Scenes from two movies bear out this point. In *The Great Debaters*, a debate team from small Wiley College, a black institution in Texas, wins a meet against Harvard's acclaimed national championship team. The topic of debate in this true story is civil disobedience. While Harvard's team presents a compelling case in favor of the rule of law, Wiley's winning argument stresses that it is not moral to obey an unjust law. By contrast, in the movie *The Hiding Place*, the Christian minister wouldn't participate in hiding Jews from the Nazis and explained his position by saying, "It's the law; and Christians must obey the law."

Jesus broke the laws that had been imposed when the religious leaders twisted God's law to say what they wanted it to say. For example, he was forever getting in trouble for doing miracles on the Sabbath. You see, the religious leaders of Jesus' day had gotten away from obeying God's laws as written *in* the Torah and instead obeyed the interpretations of those laws as written in books *about* the Torah. Sure, the Torah says to rest on the Sabbath, but it doesn't attempt to micromanage people's lives by spelling out a lengthy definition of what is meant by resting and doing no work. The interpretive books, however, do. By Jesus' day those books had gotten so specific that even good, necessary activities were restricted. So, when Jesus healed someone on the Sabbath, those leaders couldn't even see the awesome miracle because of the blinders they wore thanks to their own interpretation of what God originally had in mind. Of course it wasn't a sin to do good work on the Sabbath.

Spiritual Leaders (Pastors) Hebrews 13:17 says, "Obey your leaders and submit to their authority. They keep watch over you as men who must give an account. Obey them so that their work will be a joy, not a burden, for that would be of no advantage to you." Verse 7 of the same chapter says, "Remember your leaders, who spoke the word of God to you. Consider the outcome of their way of life and imitate their faith."

The pastor of your local congregation has been given the charge to watch over you and care for your soul. Your pastor will have to give an account before God about how he or she led and fed you. Jesus even respected God's authority that was given to spiritual leaders. In Matthew 26:62-64, Jesus is ordered by the high priest to give an answer. Jesus complies because he recognizes the man's authority as coming from God.

Although our son Matthew attends a university in our same city, he moved his membership to another church. He prefers not only the racial mix, but the higher number of young people his age. I enjoyed meeting his new pastor and have noticed that Matthew understands his pastor's role in his life, as a man to whom he should listen for sage advice and to whom he can turn when difficulties arise. In other words, Matthew knows he is responsible to obey his pastor and not be a burden to him.

If your older teen or young adult son wishes to change churches once he moves away from home or goes away to attend college, it's a good idea to talk with him about carefully avoiding bogus spiritual leaders. These types camouflage themselves by using Christian words but redefining the meanings. For example, they may use the word love to mean acceptance of every kind of lifestyle or submission to mean obedience to their warped way of thinking. A false teacher of this kind can be discovered by holding their views up to the penetrating light of the Word of God. If a pastor is adding to or taking away from the accepted Word of God, encourage your son to find another congregation.

Teachers (School Teachers, Coaches, Tutors—When Approved by Godly Parents)
The book of Proverbs has a lot to say about listening to wise advice. Look at these three verses for example:

Proverbs 12:15	Fools think their own way is right, but the wise listen to advice.
Proverbs 15:31	The ear that heeds wholesome admonition will lodge among the wise.
Proverbs 19:20	Listen to advice and accept instruction, that you may gain wisdom for the future.

These verses can be applied to teachers who should be respected and obeyed.

Teachers can have a profound influence on the lives of our sons, and they can give practical guidance. Someone like a non-Christian sports coach who teaches a good work ethic can play a valuable role.

If our sons are to become like Christ, we need to understand that teachers are examples to our sons either positively or negatively. Our boys can pick up much more than the subject being taught; they can mimic mannerisms, repeat sayings, and believe the personally held ideologies the teachers model before them.

Our son Mark was eager to play basketball once he got into high school. Coach Starr, fresh out of college and excited about leading the high school varsity team, was his new coach. Coach Starr was very cool. He was single, well-dressed, easy-going with the kids, and lots of fun. Mark stuck to Coach Starr like glue. Since the coach had just graduated from college and was temporarily living with his parents, Mark seemed to be the second son in their family. The funniest thing was how Mark picked up Coach Starr's mannerisms. Mark began to laugh like him, move like him, and even tell the same jokes. I noticed how simple it was for Mark to latch onto this teacher and was grateful that Coach Starr was a Christian man of integrity whom I could trust not to lead my son astray.

I never cease to be amazed at what an impact my own teaching has on my students. I am both elated and humbled when students return after they have graduated to tell me that something I taught them has made a difference in their lives. Wade Benjamin, now a professional personal trainer, graduated from college with a degree in behavioral science with an emphasis in sociology. He invited me to the gym where he works and proceeded to show me his client notebook (without letting me see any personal information, of course). In it were forms he had designed to keep track of everything about each person as it related to his or her fitness. Wade attributed his organizational skills to me. "I'm the only trainer here with such extensive paperwork on all my clients," he shared. "Thanks to your insistence on our keeping organized notebooks in your classes, this notebook helps me chart each client's progress and assist them so effectively that I'm the top paid trainer at both gyms where I work. I even have private clients."

Another student, David Cross, returned to tell me that he was going into the ministry. He said he wanted to thank me because my excitement in teaching Bible classes and chapel ignited his love for the Word of God and inspired him to want to share it with others.

Teachers make an impact. Be vigilant concerning whom you allow to teach your children. One reason why I believe Christian education is best for our children is that Christian schools have standards for what is to be taught, but they also have standards regarding who teaches it.

Authorities Who Want to Be Followed

Although God has given us himself, parents, spiritual leaders, and teachers, we don't always want to follow them. Let's be honest: we sometimes would much rather follow other authorities that are perhaps flashier, more up to date, or just more fun. We permit these people and things to reign in offices of authority in our lives that God has not ordained. These authority figures are like those Jesus ran into who thought they had authority but didn't really. For example, the Pharisees thought they had authority over Jesus, but he proved them wrong time and time again. Satan figured he could get Jesus to bow down to him, but Jesus thwarted his temptations by continuously citing the Word of God (see Matthew 4).

And government leaders like Herod even thought they had the power of life and death over Jesus. Our Lord let them think that was true for three days before he rose from the dead. Talk about your ultimate "Gottcha!"

If our sons will be like Christ, they must be taught to discern which authorities to follow and which ones to ignore. Would-be

Step Aside

The next time your son has a decision to make, no matter how trivial it seems, help him find Scripture that speaks to the situation. If there is absolutely no Scripture that pertains to the situation either by precept (direct command) or principle (something that can be implied from the context), then he is free to make whatever choice he would like.

Decision Faced	Scripture That Pertains to the Problem	Decision Made
Should I wear a jacket to school today?	None, unless the school has certain restrictions.	Wore the jacket.
Should I keep the money in the wallet I found?	"You shall not steal"; "Do unto others...."	Turned the money in to the police.
_____	_____	_____
_____	_____	_____
_____	_____	_____
_____	_____	_____
_____	_____	_____

authorities vying for our sons' attention are Satan, their peers, teachers and governments requiring compliance to or agreement with ungodly principles, the pull of societal norms that contradict God's Word, and their own lusts.

How will our boys know when they are being pulled by one of these ingenuous authorities? Experts who foil counterfeiters do so not by knowing what counterfeit money looks like, but by knowing well what real money looks like. When fake money shows up, they recognize it because they are so familiar with the real. In the same way, our sons will know counterfeit authorities when he is intimately familiar with God, the real authority. Model before your son and teach him how to obey God, and he will be able to spot an authority who is trying to pull him away from his core belief.

Authority over the Body

In Matthew 4 the Spirit led Jesus into the desert for the specific purpose of being tempted by the devil. Jesus put himself on a forty-day fast to face this challenge, and at the end of the forty days, obviously, he was hungry. It was then, in Jesus' weakened physical condition, that the tempter approached him, first mocking his identity and then appealing to his physical need. "If you are the Son of God," Satan jeered, "tell these stones to become bread" (Matthew 4:3). Jesus didn't even address the ridiculous insinuation that he was posing as someone he wasn't, and he maintained control over his physical body, refusing to bow to his hunger by letting himself be filled by anything Satan had to offer.

Then again, at the crucifixion, Jesus could have called legions of angels to get him out of that predicament, yet he had control over his body and would not let his physical pain overrule what he knew he had to do. In other words, his body did not overrule his mind.

Our sons, too, have to be clear about their identity and be determined to refuse to satisfy their physical needs with anything Satan has to offer. As to identity, our sons are God's gifts to us and should be told so often. As to their bodies, they must know how not to let their bodies overrule their minds.

One area of mind-body control that is out of control among young people these days is the area of sexual immorality. An amazing double standard exists. Girls are considered loose if they are promiscuous, but boys are expected to sow their wild oats. How silly that is! Who do we expect these boys to be sowing those oats with?

Let your son know that his body is a temple of the Holy Spirit (see 1 Corinthians 6:19). He has authority over his body and is responsible for keeping it pure, holy, and under control. His body is his God-given tool through which he operates and touches the world around him. If he keeps it healthy and holy, he can function at peak physical and spiritual capacity, and this is especially important as he operates in his ministry.

Besides the negative consequences connected with sexual immorality, another serious problem our sons face is childhood obesity. This is our fault as parents. Children eat what we provide for them and what we allow them to eat. We are so busy running around that we aren't concentrating on the health of our kids—that is, until they get sick. We won't have to deal with many of the problems created by childhood obesity; our children will suffer with those issues as adults. There is just no way for our boys to receive proper nutrition if we feed them a daily diet of fast-food hamburgers, fried foods, and frozen microwave quickie meals.

Take authority over your son's health for optimal results and to

Step Aside

God's Word is clear for boys, girls, men, and women. In a devotional time with your son, read each of the following Bible passages. Discuss with him the meaning of each verse and the practical ways in which he intends to obey it: Romans 6:12; 1 Corinthians 6:18; Ephesians 5:3; Colossians 3:5; 1 Thessalonians 4:3-5; 2 Timothy 2:22; 1 Peter 2:11.

enhance his proper development. You can begin to instill proper eating habits even before your son is born by feeding him properly while he is still in the womb. Expectant mothers must drink water and milk, take prenatal vitamins, and eat vegetables. New mothers should understand that all the reputable advice says that it is best to nurse infants, for that is the perfect, God-designed food for human babies. Once it is time for solid food, start infants with cereal and veggies before they are offered sweets. This will develop their taste for the healthy stuff.

Some people might have judged me as a little "over the top" when my boys were infants, but I was determined to feed them a healthy diet. I nursed them for many months and did our grocery shopping at a health food market so the boys' young systems wouldn't be filled with artificial food additives. I hope that early concentration on healthy food intake had at least a little to do with some of their later decisions. For example, Matthew decided not to eat butter because he read some literature about bad cholesterol. Since Mark is an athlete, he rarely drinks sodas, preferring juice drinks instead.

Step Aside

As your son grows, remain involved in his food choices. After the examples below, list some healthy changes you can make.

■ Keep fruit, raw vegetables, nuts, and cereals available as snacks instead of cookies, cupcakes, and candy.

_____

_____

_____

■ Serve water with dinner and prepare balanced lunches and dinners.

_____

_____

_____

■ Be sure your son eats breakfast.

_____

_____

_____

9
The Gentleman Relating to Women

The connection between mother and son is a boy's first relationship with a woman, and in some cases it is a woman's first experience of totally unconditional love from a man. After all, this involves much more than emotion. A very real physical attachment exists with biological sons.

Being pregnant fascinated me. I was awed to think that inside of me, attached and growing, was another human being, totally and completely dependent on me for his very survival. The air I breathed, the food I consumed, the stress I encountered—all transferred to and affected that innocent little life. By the day of his birth, our relationship was already nine months old. When my baby suckled at my breasts, he was comforted to find that his physical severance from my body was not a cold-turkey separation from his connection to me. In the early weeks and months of each son's life, his slightest uneasiness caused him to crave only the comfort that his mother's arms—my arms—could and would gladly provide.

This raw, unblemished, and totally natural love is the reason some fathers become jealous of their wives' relationship with their infant sons. By nature, the bond forged between mothers and sons is special, different from, and I would venture to say, possibly even stronger than other human bonds.

Boys love their mamas. When you hear someone talking negatively about a boy's mother, "dem's fightin' words." A verbal confrontation will immediately escalate to a fistfight when one boy utters the most forbidden phrase, "Your mama." He probably never had to fight for her honor, but I'm sure that just such an exceptionally special bond existed between Jesus and his mother.

Respect for Women—Jesus and His Mother

Jesus showed his mother respect, so a son who respects his mother is already like Christ in this regard. Let's see how Jesus lived out the bond he had with his mother.

We already discussed in chapter 2 about twelve-year-old Jesus staying behind at the temple instead of joining the caravan to go back home. Please pick up from that story how Jesus respected his mother. Both Mary and Joseph had been frantically searching for him, but Mary was the one who voiced her concern and relief when they found him. "Son, why have you treated us like this? Your father and I have been anxiously searching for you" (Luke 2:48).

Although Mary didn't fully understand Jesus' comment about being in his Father's house, she treasured in her heart how he answered and the fact that he obeyed her anyway. Luke 2:51 says, "Then he went down to Nazareth with them and was obedient to them."

As Jesus matured, his specialness wasn't lost on Mary. A mother knows her child. In time she realized that his obedience to her was a clear sign of his voluntary submission. He continued to respect his mother and to submit to her after he was an adult. In fact, his first miracle was at Mary's request (see John 2:1-11).

Later in his ministry though, it seems as if Jesus rudely ignored his mother. In Matthew 12:47, Jesus was heavily involved in ministry when Mary and his brothers showed up where he was speaking, desiring an audience with him. He seemed to refuse to see them, replying instead, "'Who is my mother, and who are my brothers?' Pointing to his disciples, he said, 'Here are my mother and my brothers.

For whoever does the will of my Father in heaven is my brother and sister and mother'" (Matthew 12:48-50). At first glance Jesus' behavior sure seems cold, but I see in this incident a sign of respect too. Jesus respected his mother by respecting the calling she had helped raise him to fulfill. He was under obligation to do what he was called by God to do, even if that meant not seeing her as much.

Now, many of you reading this book have very young sons, so you may not feel that the following example will apply to you for a long time, but just hang in there with me; I promise I'm going somewhere. One of my friends wrote me an e-mail just before Easter saying that she had to prepare the holiday dinner for about sixteen people. The number included her newly married son, Shaun, and his new wife who had decided at the last minute to join them for the feast. If she had known they were going to attend, she wouldn't have invited the others, because now that Shaun was married, she didn't get a chance to spend much time with him. She jokingly wished our traditions matched that of another society's in which the son and daughter-in-

Step Aside

The following are ways to prepare yourself for the day your son must leave either for college, marriage, the military, or job relocation.

- Start talking to your son about college when he is in kindergarten. These are casual conversations about school and how one grade leads to another.
- Allow your son to spend the night with friends at homes where you know and approve of the parents' lifestyles. Invite those friends for overnighters at your house too.
- While in later elementary school, let your son attend summer camp for one- or two-week experiences away from home.
- During high school, encourage your son to participate in summer projects with mission groups or at universities where he can get a head start on his college interests.

law moved in with the son's parents and the daughter-in-law did all the housework.

My friend was teasing, but I felt the point of her joke. She missed Shaun. She had enjoyed the job she was assigned to fulfill as his mother and had relished every moment of his upbringing. Those precious days were gone forever, and she was feeling a certain sadness about that. Nevertheless, if we will raise sons who will respect us, we must rear them to know that we understand both our role and theirs in the dance called the passage of time. We must teach them to lead, so by default, we must step out of that spot. Shaun isn't supposed to live under his mom's roof his whole life. He has done the right thing by "leaving and cleaving," but his mom, although sincerely happy about that, still misses him from time to time.

As we seek to raise our sons to be like Christ, we must realize that that means eventually setting them free to be all that God wants them to be. A son's relationship with his mother can either nurture him toward godly maturity or severely stunt his spiritual growth. It is all a matter of how a mother handles the issue of respect.

Respect is a product of the proper balance between discipline, love, and trust. Sons respect mothers whom they can trust to be consistent both in discipline and in love. They respect mothers who love them enough to make them secure, discipline them enough to make them strong, and trust them and God enough to let them go. A mother trains her son, saying, "You will grow up to be a man," and then trusts him, letting go of the reins so he can actually start being a man when he reaches adulthood. Jesus likely showed so much respect for his mother because she had mastered this balancing act.

And we see the final result of Jesus' utter love and deep respect for his mother when, as he was dying on the cross, he used some of his precious last breaths to take care of her and to affirm that she had raised him to do what he had to do. John 19:25-27 relates the touching scene.

Near the cross of Jesus stood his mother, his mother's sister, Mary the wife of Clopas, and Mary Magdalene. When Jesus saw his mother there, and the disciple whom he loved standing nearby, he said to his mother, "Dear woman, here is your son," and to the disciple, "Here is your mother." From that time on, this disciple took her into his home.

The following verse of the above passage begins by saying, "Later, knowing that all was now completed . . ." (John 19:28). Do you catch that? In other words, in his extreme agony, while the weight of the sins of the world pressed in on him as the Son of God, Jesus remembered he was Mary's Son too. Everything was not accomplished until he had taken care of his mother. That's love. That's respect. That's amazing.

A word of caution though to keep everything in perspective: we mothers are not supposed to be in the business of raising our sons so that they will take care of us when they are grown. Quite the contrary. As is the main point above, we are supposed to be raising them to take care of themselves and their families. If we are handling things right as parents, we should be leaving an inheritance for our children's children" (Proverbs 13:22). If we are able to leave an inheritance for our grandchildren, that means we must have enough to take care of ourselves. The fact that our sons will turn around and be sure their mothers are cared for is not a function of duty, but one of respect that flows from a heart of love.

"But what of this business of letting my son go?" you ask. "Exactly how am I supposed to bring myself to that point? Holding this little bundle or watching him play with his friends, smile, and bring me wilted wildflowers, it just doesn't seem like I'll ever be able to let him go." I know how you feel; however, we have to come to a place where we are determined to do what we must, not what feels good. Let's get some letting-go help from another biblical mom.

Moses' mother gives us a prime example of a woman who let go of her son, trusting him into God's hands. While her precious son was just an infant, she prepared a little ark for him and placed him in the Nile River, hoping and praying it would carry him to safety. To get the full story, read Exodus 1:7-22, where the account is given of how the Egyptian pharaoh planned to kill all the male Hebrew babies by tossing them into the Nile. The very location pharaoh planned to use for extermination, God used for preservation.

We, too, are asked to "place our sons in the Nile." The world into which they must venture can be a brutal place. Our job is to prepare

---

Step Aside

Seek to balance discipline, love, and trust. For two weeks, keep track of the words of discipline (correction, criticism, advice) that proceed from your mouth. Are these words balanced with words of love and actions of trust? All three won't necessarily happen at the same time, but at the end of the day, do the scales balance?

Words/Actions of Discipline	Words/Actions of Love	Words/Actions of Trust
"No TV until your homework is finished."	Give him a hug as he passes by.	"Call when you get to your friend's house"
_____	_____	_____
_____	_____	_____
_____	_____	_____
_____	_____	_____
_____	_____	_____
_____	_____	_____
_____	_____	_____

---

sturdy arks of safety for them ahead of time. We do this in many ways. We can provide a secure family life for them and teach them godly viewpoints on such issues as education, sex, and choosing friends wisely. Living godly lifestyles before them will make an impact as well, as will encouraging them to trust God for themselves by teaching them to pray and read the Bible.

I felt I was in the same predicament as Moses' mom. This world would just as soon throw my sons "into the river" than hear their testimony and see them live lives that glorify God. As I read through those first chapters of Exodus, I watched how Moses' mother handled the situation and found guidance for raising my boys.

Responsibility toward Women—
Jesus and Women in Need

In an Internet article titled "Men Protecting Women," author Frederica Mathewes-Green observes: "It's part of the guy job description. Whenever there's danger, any man is expected to protect any woman at any cost. This is true no matter who she is; it's not an honor awarded only to his wife or daughter. . . . It's just what we expect men to do."[1]

This discussion reminds me of a debate that took place one day in a senior English high school class I was teaching. When the subject of male-female interaction came up, the guys strongly rejected the notion that girls should be allowed to do all the same things guys do. They used football as an example. The guys believed that allowing women into the National Football League would ruin the game. Why? Because men would always treat women with more care. They wouldn't hit as hard or play as vigorously if women were on the teams. Even after I laid out a hypothetical situation including a female player with all the same height, weight, and experience as a male, the boys refused to change their position.

"But why, then," I asked, "would you treat the female player any differently?"

Their emphatic and immediate answer came in unison: "Because she's a girl, and men are supposed to protect girls."

Others besides Mathewes-Green and my students seem to feel the same way. I found a Yahoo blog that asked, "Do you think men have a responsibility to protect women from getting hurt?" Blogs are used by people all over the world as a means of venting one's opinions. Judging by the pictures of themselves people had posted, the respondents to this particular blog seemed to be young adults in their twenties. In a society that places a premium on tolerance and women's liberation, I expected this crowd to respond negatively. However, overwhelmingly, the answer was yes. One young woman's representative answer was, "It's a guy's instinct to protect women. I think it's somewhere inside of every man to be strong and courageous and hero-like." The majority of the men who answered agreed that being responsible to protect women was instinctive.

Speaking, then, from the perspective of our modern-day culture, I guess we would categorize Jesus as a typical guy in this regard. He shows us, through his responses to the needy women around him, that it is both a guy thing and a godly thing to act responsibly toward women, to help them when they are in need. And Jesus modeled for our boys just how they were to do this.

Let's look at three women who needed something from Jesus. In noticing how he responded to them, we can gain some insight into how we can direct our sons to be like Christ in their responses to the women with whom they come in contact.

John 8:1-11 relates the tension-filled story of the woman caught in adultery. The woman's disingenuous accusers orchestrated the whole episode to trap Jesus in a disagreement with Moses' teaching. Jesus ignored the challenge and focused on the woman. Verse 7 contains his only response to the dishonest bunch: "If any one of you is without sin, let him be the first to throw a stone at her." One by one, from the oldest to the youngest, her accusers left the scene. Then Jesus' attention turned back to the woman. John wraps up the story like this:

Jesus straightened up and asked her, "Woman, where are they? Has no one condemned you?"

"No one, sir," she said. "Then neither do I condemn you," Jesus declared. "Go now and leave your life of sin."

Notice what Jesus did for this embarrassed woman. First, he confronted her accusers. He dealt with those who were causing her discomfort. Then he refused to condemn her, encouraged her to leave her life of sin, and affirmed her hopeful future.

Boys who will be like Christ in their treatment of women will always defend a woman's honor. A woman caught in a compromising position clearly knows her plight. There is no need for her protector to remind her of it too. What is needed is protection and encouragement to go on from there.

The second biblical woman's story we will look at is that of the Samaritan woman whom Jesus met at a well just outside her town. During a conversation that surprised this woman (Jews and Samaritans loathed each other), Jesus listened to her as if she were an intelligent human being and then answered her based on what she had said to him. He acknowledged her intelligence even though he had another viewpoint. Then he asked her to do for him only what she was able to do. He offered her the best he had to give (living water), and this supplied her with a reason to tell others about him. (Read the whole story in John 4:4-30, 39-42.)

Boys will be like Christ when they treat women as intelligent human beings. They will not expect women to be who they are not, nor will they require women to do for them what they are incapable of doing. When it comes to dealing with their wives, our sons will be like Christ when they give the best they have to give.

A third woman Jesus encountered and helped is Mary Magdalene. Interestingly, the Bible does not give us a detailed account of how she came to be delivered by Jesus. In a seeming afterthought in Mark 16:9, we are told that Jesus cast seven demons out of her. This fact seems to have become insignificant to the Gospel writers because the

Step Aside

From the above discussion, let's pull out three dos and three don'ts that relate to how boys/young men should treat girls/young women. Beside each entry is one suggestion about how to live this out in a practical way. Add more ideas of your own.

Boys/Young men should:

■ Defend a woman's honor: Do not let a girl be bullied on the playground.

_____

_____

■ Treat women as intelligent human beings: Listen with a view to understand a young lady's point of view when having a discussion.

_____

_____

■ Give the best they have to give: In a relationship with a woman, be honest and conduct yourself at your highest standard.

_____

_____

Boys/Young men should not:

■ Expect a woman to be who she is not: Honor the godly morals a female friend has set for herself.

_____

_____

■ Require women to do what they are incapable of doing: Do not expect your wife to be your mother.

_____

_____

■ Victimize women: Do not use your strength to force a woman to do what you want her to do.

_____

_____

numerous other mentions of her focus on her service to the Master and on the fact that Jesus appeared to her first after his resurrection (see Matthew 28:5-11; John 20:1-2; 11-18).

So what did Jesus do for Mary Magdalene, a woman who had been severely victimized? Besides casting the demons out of her, he personally assuaged her anguish. I believe that being the first one to see Jesus as the risen Lord was her reward for selflessly serving him from the time she met him. In other words, Jesus was there for Mary; he had her back. He also gave her a joyous assignment. She was the one given the charge to go and tell the disciples that he was alive.

Boys who will treat women as Christ treated women will never be the victimizers, but will instead take the responsibility for comforting women who have been victimized.

Response to Women

Respect for all females shapes a male's responses to individual women. A boy who is raised to respect the girls around him, such as his sisters and little friends, will later respect the women in his life, such as his wife and daughters. The opposite is also true, as depicted in the classic Dickens novel *A Tale of Two Cities*. Dickens points out the negative side of this truth through two minor characters, Jerry Cruncher and his young son. The senior Jerry hates it when his wife prays for him, and he shows his scorn in his son's presence by verbally abusing her and throwing his muddy boots at her. Young Jerry follows his father's deplorable example in his disrespect for his mother.

A primary way that disrespect for women is promulgated today is through rap music, which exerts a huge influence over young people. Some rap music, liked and played incessantly by many young men, denigrates women, boldly and unashamedly calling them filthy names and portraying vile scenarios. The lyrics preach a philosophy that sees women mainly as playthings and sex objects. Young models, hoping to get their big break in the music business, play right into the hands of the disrespectful composers by gyrating in front of video cameras that record visual versions of these songs. The resulting DVDs vividly depict the misogynistic messages that go on to be burned into the minds and psyches of young men.

My friend Diana is raising two teenage boys. Alarmed by what her sons were seeing on the rap videos, she sat them down to have a discussion about it. She told them that those girls were someone's daughters and sisters. She explained that she was no different than those girls in that respect. She was their grandfather's daughter and their uncle's sister. Then Diana got up and started dancing like the girls on the DVDs. Her sons quickly stopped her, yelling, "Mommy, don't!" They got the point.

Boys who would become like Christ must be challenged to seriously evaluate their musical choices. GIGO—garbage in, garbage out. Even though boys will argue that they are only listening to the music, don't buy that for one minute. Most of the young people I have encountered over my twenty-six-year teaching career can readily quote more rap lyrics than Scripture, so the words are breaking through somehow.

One closing note must be shared here about our sons' dealings with women. Once they reach adolescence, the sex question becomes uppermost in boys' minds. Suddenly you notice that your son, whom you practically had to wrestle into the bathtub each night, is voluntarily taking several showers a day and dousing himself in his dad's cologne. Lo and behold, he has discovered girls, and girls have discovered him. This starts earlier in the lives of some boys than others, but sooner or later, it will happen.

My son Mark has always been a ladies' man. From the time he could talk, he naturally noticed a new hairdo, bright

Step Aside

Sit with your son and listen to the music he likes. Discuss the meaning of the lyrics and then allow him to justify why, as a Christian young man, he should listen to that particular artist. Ask him if he thinks Jesus would listen to those songs on his radio or iPod.

lipstick, or beautiful jewelry and would compliment me or other women without any prompting. Girls starting calling our house for him when he was in the first grade. This point is especially important for guys like Mark.

The commandments about abstinence apply to boys as well as girls. Respect for women extends into the sexual arena. A young man is respecting a young woman when he does not ask her to disobey God and have sex with him before they are married. If he will grow to be a responsible husband, he can start by being a responsible boyfriend, through obedience to 1 Corinthians 6:18, "Flee from sexual immorality. All other sins a man commits are outside his body, but he who sins sexually sins against his own body."

We are usually very adamant with our girls about maintaining their virginity until marriage, but God intends for our boys to be virgins when they marry too. We are not giving our sons godly advice if we tell them it is okay to sow their wild oats.

NOTE
1. NPR, All Things Considered, "Men Protecting Women", Posted Wednesday, October 9, 1996, in Marriage and Family, Gender. http://www.frederica.com, Frederica Mathewes-Green.

Step Aside

Do not be afraid to talk with your son about sex. He needs to know both the biological and the spiritual truth. If you need help breaching the topic with your son, I recommend True Love Waits. This is a program that challenges teenagers and college students to make a commitment to sexual abstinence until marriage. Their website says, "True Love Waits is designed to encourage moral purity by adhering to biblical principles. This youth-based international campaign utilizes positive peer pressure by encouraging those who make a commitment to refrain from pre-marital sex to challenge their peers to do the same." Check them out at www.lifeway.com/tlw/.

10
The Manager Handling Money

In an *Our Daily Bread* devotion titled "Money and Time," the writer said: "At some point, it struck me that both money and time have been very important commodities as far back as anyone can remember. Yet they present one of the great dilemmas of life. We trade our valuable time working for money, and then we spend our money to make the most of our time off. We seldom possess the two with any degree of balance."[1] Many times, our relationship to money rules our lives and reveals much about us. Extremes either way—caring too much about money or not caring enough—get us into trouble. The balancing act is often quite precarious and is even one of the main causes of family rifts, friendships ending, and divorces.

Jesus' views on money offer the balanced view we need to teach to our sons. Once they catch his vision, they will be another step closer to living as reflections of his image.

Lets' start with the Sermon on the Mount, Jesus' manifesto of the kingdom. In this premiere sermon, Jesus sets forth important guidelines about such things as anger, divorce, oaths, fasting, and prayer, among other things. In Matthew 6:24, he begins a discussion about what our overall attitude toward money should be: "No one can serve two masters. Either he will hate the one and love the other, or he will be devoted to the one and despise the other. You cannot serve both God and Money." Jesus goes on to explain that God knows we need food and clothes, and he will take care of those needs as we put him first. In other words, our attitude toward money should be one that says, "Yes, I realize I need money for things, but first and foremost, I need to focus on how God wants me to live. As long as I'm doing that, God will supply my earthly needs." Since commerce is the main manner by which we receive goods and services, a proper focus on God will mean receiving his direction in how to handle the money that will bring those earthly needs our way.

Luke's gospel connects this same teaching to a parable Jesus taught about a dishonest manager. This guy had been playing fast and loose with the boss's money and got caught. Knowing he would soon be confronted and probably fired, he figured he had to do something to hedge himself when he was out and needing to deal with other people. He approached the people who owed him money and offered them a discount so he would have what he needed when he faced his boss. Upon hearing that the manager had done this, the boss was impressed. Jesus goes on from this parable to teach the following financial lesson:

> "I tell you, use worldly wealth to gain friends for yourselves, so that when it is gone, you will be welcomed into eternal dwellings.
>
> "Whoever can be trusted with very little can also be trusted with much, and whoever is dishonest with very little will also be dishonest with much. So if you have not been trustworthy in handling worldly wealth, who will trust you with true riches? And if you have not been trustworthy with someone else's property, who will give you property of your own?
>
> "No servant can serve two masters. Either he will hate the one and love the other, or he will be devoted to the one and despise the other. You cannot serve both God and Money." (Luke 16:9-13)

Verse 9 is a little perplexing. It seems, however, that Jesus is telling us that we can prepare for a warm reception in heaven by making good use of our possessions in this world. We should use what we have to honor God by providing generously for others. Of course, good deeds can't buy eternal rewards, but believers who show by their deeds that they have been changed by Christ will be rewarded in heaven.

Jesus intends for our sons to have a healthy attitude toward money, one that is neither miserly nor irresponsible. The best way to raise a boy who is responsible with his money is to model that responsibility yourself.

Sometimes we are so busy telling our sons to stay out of trouble that we neglect to tell them exactly how to accomplish that goal. For example, we tell our boys not to give in to peer pressure, but we rarely take the time to tell them how to accomplish that. We have discussed the proper attitude toward money; now let's explore four major negatives Jesus taught about wealth in an effort to glean some principles to teach our sons about how to maintain that proper attitude. The four negatives Jesus wants us to know are: *wealth is deceitful*, *wealth can deny you of God's blessings*, *wealth can derail your ministry*, and *wealth can dim your judgment*.

Wealth Is Deceitful

In the parable of the sower (Matthew 13:1-23; Luke 8:5-15), Jesus teaches us about the different ways in which the Word of God is received. Sometimes the Word of God does not affect a person's life as it should, because it is choked out by the deceitfulness of wealth. Money deludes us into thinking that chasing after it is more important than chasing after God. We become inordinately worried about and tangled up with life's worries and life's pleasures, both of which involve money. All our concentration focuses on this life, which is fleeting, instead of on the next, which is eternal.

Notice that Jesus never said the problem is wealth in and of itself. The problem is the deceitfulness of wealth, the slick way our needs turn to greed and the craving for ever more wealth slides into our mind and consumes us. You can teach your son to short-circuit this subtle tilt out of balance by encouraging him to incorporate biblical principles into his financial life. Concentrating on what God wants him to do with his money will take the burden of worry about money off of him.

There are four main biblical principles that can lead your son not only to a balanced view of wealth, but also to financial freedom. These four principles are *tithing, giving, saving,* and *living within one's means.*

Principle number one is *tithing.* The tithe represents 10 percent of all of your increase. Proverbs 3:9 tells us that we honor the Lord by giving him what belongs to him first. Abraham paid tithes to Melchizedek, the priest of the most high God, way back in Genesis (see 14:18-20), so this is not just some practice we can overlook as some old relic of the Mosaic law. Malachi 3:10 commands us to "Bring the whole tithe into the storehouse" so that not only the needs of God's house will be met, but so that blessings will pour out on us as well.

Closely related to principle one, is principle number two, *giving.* A giving heart reflects Christ's image perfectly. After all, as we know from the most popular Scripture passage in the world, God loved the world so much that he gave his Son to save it (see John 3:16). We will talk more about the practical aspects of tithing and giving in the next section.

Principle number three is *saving.* We will have nothing to give unless we incorporate a habit of saving into our financial plan. The Bible even tells us that we should have

Step Aside
What is your son's overall attitude about money? His attitude probably reflects yours. Does he hoard it or spend it frivolously, or are his actions somewhere in between those two?

enough stored away that there will be something from us for our grandchildren.

Principle number four is *living within our means*. Many of us have experienced the stress of having more month than money when we have racked up credit card bills we have to struggle to pay. Credit is such a deceptive thing, especially for our sons when they become college students. The credit card companies target these new adults with an abundance of freedom. College freshmen are offered credit cards, and once they receive them, those first few months are pure bliss. They whip out their cards at retail stores and restaurants, sign their names, and enjoy the benefits. Not one dime exchanges hands. But oh the pain at the end of several billing cycles when they realize that paying that minimum payment rarely affects the total balance, thanks of course to those pesky interest rates.

My friend Pat's son, Craig, faced this all-too-common problem, as did our Matthew. As a film major in college, Matthew justified using his cards to produce his movies. When outside financing to reimburse him didn't materialize as he supposed it would, he got stuck with the bills. Couple that decision with some spending on other items he felt he needed to keep up with the lifestyle of the film industry, and he found himself in a financial crunch out of which he must now dig himself.

Step Aside

As soon as your son starts earning money—be it his allowance, payment from neighbors for errands or odd jobs, or his actual paycheck—teach him to live by the 70–30 principle. For every amount of money he takes in, have him tithe 10 percent, save 10 percent, put aside 10 percent for giving, and live off of the 70 percent that is left. His savings is his long-term investment for big-ticket items, such as college, a car, a home, and retirement. His giving account is for blessing others. This money is not to be used as loans, but as gifts bestowed prayerfully and maybe even anonymously.

In Craig's case Pat relates that he too had never had a credit card until he went to college. Then, as a freshman, he became submerged in debt. He joined the Marines and was unreachable for four years. When he got out, he applied for a school loan, and guess what? That credit card debt was there waiting for him. He made arrangements to pay off his debt, but all those years unpaid did a number on his credit rating.

An important lesson to teach our sons is to live within their means. The writer of Hebrews puts it this way, "Keep your lives free from the love of money and be content with what you have, because God has said, 'Never will I leave you; never will I forsake you.' So we say with confidence, 'The Lord is my helper; I will not be afraid. What can man do to me?'" (Hebrews 13:5-6). Since God is the one helping your son manage his finances wisely, your son won't have to worry about men coming after him with threats, judgments, repossessions, and foreclosures. His financial business will be straight, his dealings honest, his credit A-1, his needs met, and even some of his wants enjoyed debt-free.

Wealth Can Deny You God's Blessing

In Luke 6:38, Jesus says, "Give, and it will be given to you. A good measure, pressed down, shaken together and running over, will be poured into your lap. For with the measure you use, it will be measured to you." Jesus is actually speaking in this passage of what we can expect when we withhold judgment and condemnation and instead forgive liberally. The principle seems to apply for giving liberally as well. If we readily forgive those who bring an offense against us, not only will God be faithful to forgive us time and again, but he will give us favor among others. Likewise, if we give to others when they need help, God will use others to give liberally to us when we are in need. Those who sow plentifully will reap plentifully.

Do you see how wealth can deny you of God's blessing? The word *give* in Luke 6:38 is in the present imperative tense, which means it is a command to do something today. Obedience to this command will bring about reciprocal return; disobedience will bring the opposite. So, if your son has wealth and refuses to be a giver, he can expect two things: first, people will not be giving toward him, and second, God will not be giving to him. Hoarding his wealth will therefore deny him of God's blessing.

I mentioned Malachi 3:10 above, but the whole passage continues to point out the blessing attached to tithing.

> "Bring the whole tithe into the storehouse, that there may be food in my house. Test me in this," says the LORD Almighty, "and see if I will not throw open the floodgates of heaven and pour out so much blessing that you will not have room enough for it. I will prevent pests from devouring your crops, and the vines in your fields will not cast their fruit," says the LORD Almighty. "Then all the nations will call you blessed, for yours will be a delightful land," says the LORD Almighty.

You would be right in questioning the sanity of your son if he refused such a generous offer from almighty God. Look at what God is saying. He says to trust him enough to test tithing out. He says that if we tithe, he will throw open heaven's treasuries and pour out so much blessing that we won't even have room enough to receive it all. Not only that, but he will also protect the stuff we do have, blessing us to such an extent that it's obvious to outsiders.

My friend Joseph was a staunch believer in the blessings of tithing and had modeled tithing in the home as his son Glynn was growing up. Now a man living on his own, Glynn refuses to tithe; however, he is constantly concerned about having enough money to make ends meet. Every time Glynn gets ahead a little financially, something happens to pull him back down. He is sabotaging his own finances. Without God's protection over the things he has, he continues to experience periodic leaks in his bucket when the car breaks down, the refrigerator goes out, the dishwasher stops running, or hours are unexpectedly cut back at work.

Challenge your son to tithe and give. Teach him to do both because he loves and trusts God. It may be a little hard not to think about it, but the blessings are a natural outcome. Remember that God is sovereign. Blessings will come in many forms, not always as money. Health, peace, friendships, safety, opportunities, a sound mind—all of these are blessings from God.

Wealth Can Derail Your Ministry

The word *ministry* refers to the act of serving. A minister is defined as a person acting for another as an agent and carrying out given orders or designs. As Christians, our whole lives are to be lived as agents carrying out God's orders; therefore, everything we are involved in as Christians is ministry.

One of the most regrettable accounts in Scripture is that of a young man who missed out on his ministry because of his riches. We read about this rich young ruler's encounter with Jesus in Matthew 19:16-24. He approached Jesus wondering what good thing there was he could do to get eternal life. Jesus cut to the core of the man's real concern by focusing on the word "good." This guy was really after affirmation that what he was already doing was good enough to get him into heaven. Jesus played along, setting the challenge by telling him to obey the commandments. Jesus rattled off a partial list, and the fellow thought he had it made because he figured he was already doing all of the ones Jesus named. The man then asked the question that brought him to the end of himself: "What do I still lack?" Jesus responded with the one thing the young ruler didn't expect to hear: "If you want to be perfect, go, sell your possessions and give to the poor, and you will have treasure in heaven. Then come, follow me."

What is so regrettable about this story is found in verse 22: "When the young man heard this, he went away sad, because he had great wealth." This fellow's wealth kept him from following

Jesus. This is the only record in Scripture of a person being personally invited to become Jesus' disciple and declining the invitation. We could possibly have been reading a gospel or an epistle written by this guy, but he allowed his money to keep him from ministry.

Caution your son against the thirst for money, for it can keep him from following the voice of God. Although those who labor for the kingdom of God are worthy to be paid well, service vocations do not usually offer the salary and fringe benefits offered by corporate America. Most preachers and teachers aren't getting rich from their jobs.

The love of money can also keep your son from taking care of his ministry to his family. Marriage and parenting require a substantial financial commitment on the part of any adult. Hoarding money needed for the family and misusing funds needed for the family are both wrong. The misuse or abuse of money can derail a marriage. We must raise our sons to understand financial responsibility so that they will keep this area of their family life balanced.

One of my friends told me that when their twenty-year-old son received his first paycheck after being unemployed for months, he went out and blew through it in a matter of days.

Step Aside

Think of a little business your young son can operate. It may be a Kool-Aid stand like the one Matthew had, or it may be something else, such as a neighborhood cleanup service. If initial supplies are needed, you can invest, but be sure your son realizes that your investment is a loan that his business is responsible to pay back. Whatever supplies he needs from then on are to come from his profits. Help him to set the prices for his goods or services at fair market value, taking into consideration his desire to reap a profit over his costs. Insist that he keep accurate records. Set an initial time limit, maybe a month to start, during which his business must be run. Evaluate the success or failure of the business at the end of the stated interval.

She and her husband noticed that the same thing happened with his second paycheck. As the third paycheck approached, they discussed the fact that their son needed to pay rent in order to live at home. When her husband told her how much he was going to charge their son, she thought the amount was way too high. Her husband countered, saying, "I want him to learn to pinch pennies. If we charge too little, he'll never learn to save his money. We have to prepare him for what life is really like."

Another way money can derail your son's ministry is if he doesn't handle his business transactions properly, especially when dealing with taxes. In Mark 12:14-17 when Jesus was asked whether it was right to pay taxes, he answered, "Give to Caesar what is Caesar's and to God what is God's."

You can start early teaching your son to take care of business. When Matthew was about seven years old, he operated a Kool-Aid, chips, and resale toy business. I have a picture of him sitting out on the front lawn behind his little table covered with ziplock bags of chips, a pitcher of Kool-Aid, and a stack of Styrofoam cups. A handmade two-tier shelf is beside him laden with small used toys priced to sell. Mark was the advertising executive who stood near the curb flagging down cars to bring in buyers. I required Matthew to keep a ledger documenting his profits and balancing that against his costs. The business only ran about a month because Matthew did not see the profit he had expected. One of the biggest lessons he learned is that it takes money to make money. Chips, Kool-Aid, sugar, ziplock bags, and cups ate up most of his profit.

Wealth Will Dim Your Judgment

Finally, make your son aware that an unbalanced relationship with money will dim his judgment. Proverbs 30:8-9 makes this plain: "Keep falsehood and lies far from me; give me neither poverty nor riches, but give me only my daily bread. Otherwise, I may have too much and disown you and say, 'Who is the LORD?' Or I may become poor and steal, and so dishonor the name of my God." Our attitude toward money is directly related to our relationship with it and our view of it. If we get into situations where we are functioning at the extremes, our judgment will be clouded. Too much wealth can lead us to disown God; poverty can cause us to dishonor God.

Jesus showed us how he felt about an unbalanced view of money when he cleared the temple of those who sold and bought there, those who took advantage of people in need who had come there for a spiritual uplift (see Matthew 21:12-13; Mark 11:15-17). Those sellers were concerned only with making a buck. That's poor judgment.

Jesus chided the teachers of the law and the Pharisees for having a warped sense of value. In Matthew 23:16-17, he rebuked them saying, "Woe to you, blind guides! You say, 'If anyone swears by the temple, it means nothing; but if anyone swears by the gold of the temple, he is bound by his oath.' You blind fools! Which is greater: the gold, or the temple that makes the gold sacred?" These men held positions of spiritual leadership, yet they placed more value on the gold that covered the temple than on what the temple stood for. That's poor judgment.

When our sons are not taught sound financial principles, they will not understand the value of money or the role money should play in their lives. This will lead to making poor choices—bad judgments—as soon as they get their hands on some money. As in earlier examples, they may make poor choices with credit cards or spend their paychecks on

Step Aside

An exercise that can help your son understand the value of money is to allow him to help with the monthly bills. Give him a powerful visual of where money goes in your home.

- Instead of depositing your paycheck, have it cashed in relatively small bills.
- Clear off a table and set out your bills.
- Pay each bill by counting out the cash that covers each account.

frivolous things. Receiving too much too soon and too easily almost always leads to poor judgment.

Closing Thoughts on Money

Paul, the apostle who wrote most of the New Testament, knew Jesus' heart regarding many issues, including money. Listening to his instruction to Timothy regarding wealth is a great way to put a period on this chapter.

> People who want to get rich fall into temptation and a trap and into many foolish and harmful desires that plunge men into ruin and destruction. For the love of money is a root of all kinds of evil. Some people, eager for money, have wandered from the faith and pierced themselves with many griefs. . . .
>
> Command those who are rich in this present world not to be arrogant nor to put their hope in wealth, which is so uncertain, but to put their hope in God, who richly provides us with everything for our enjoyment. (1 Timothy 6:9-10, 17)

Our sons will do well to heed these words.

NOTE

1. David McCasland, "Money and Time," *Our Daily Bread*, March 9, 2004, http://www.rbc.org/devotionals/our-daily-bread/2004/03/09/devotion.aspx.

11
The Friend at the Death of Lazarus

People fear death for many different reasons—the unknown, the process leading to death, the question of what will happen to loved ones left behind, not to mention the fear of possibly missing heaven. Juxtaposed to these fears about death stand our bodies totally geared for survival, geared to stay away from death at all costs. The body heals itself and protects itself, and thanks to adrenalin, that good old fight-or-flight response keeps us on our toes.

God's Word calls death an enemy; in fact, death is so foreboding it is the last enemy that will be defeated (1 Corinthians 15:26). This enemy invades not only our physical lives, but our emotional lives as well. Yes, people die, but dreams die, relationships die, and even our character can die.

Can Jesus identify with the way we experience death? Scripture doesn't tell us that Jesus ever attended a funeral. He didn't even stay dead himself. Death couldn't last when he was around; however, in our lives, death, as well as many other negative experiences, is an unfortunate reality.

Remember the point of this book. We are training our sons to understand that they are not the starting point. They are learning to avoid saying, "Jesus, here's what I'm going through; now handle it." Instead, we are teaching them to steadfastly turn their eyes upon

Jesus and make him the starting point for their behavior. We are helping them to build a habit of saying, "Jesus, what did you do that can show me what I should do?"

Jesus indeed dealt with death and negative circumstances. If our sons are to be like Christ, they can observe him in crisis and learn how to handle their bad times with the same grace with which he handled his. So exactly how did Jesus cope with the deaths of those around him?

Handling the Death of a Friend

One day Jesus received a message that his friend Lazarus was sick. You would think Jesus would have gone to be with his friend as soon as possible, but instead, Jesus stayed where he was for two more days. That sounds kind of cruel, especially since everybody knew Jesus could heal people. But if you read the account in John 11, you will notice that Jesus planned to do something very special in this case. It makes perfect sense that Jesus would choose Lazarus to raise from the dead. After all, don't we all do extra-special things for our friends? As Jesus' good friend, Lazarus received the privilege of not just being healed like the strangers in the crowds were, but he would forever hold the distinction of being the one Jesus called back to life after being dead for four whole days (see v. 39).

Unfortunately, too many of our sons are living in communities in which drive-by shootings, campus killings, gang initiation murders, and general mayhem are the norm rather than the exception. Far too many young men have experienced attending the funerals of their buddies—lives cut short long before they should have been. Prolonged exposure to this kind of lifestyle causes a sense of desperation and hopelessness in some young men. The defense mechanism against this kind of despair is a callous attitude. It hurts too much to care or have hope when loved ones keep dying and dreams are constantly being extinguished. This is why we find young men in the prime of life believing they won't live past age twenty anyway, so there is no real need to plan for the future or care about today. These young men may gravitate toward gangs that give them immediate acceptance, perceived protection, and a sense of purpose, although temporary and fleeting. Some may choose drugs that at least temporarily suspend the hopelessness and crush the pain they feel. Still others may decide sexual promiscuity is in order. Their motto: "Have fun now, because I could very well be dead tomorrow."

Reaching young men who have sunk to this level of despondency will take a concerted effort on the part of families, communities, churches, and government organizations. Turning these boys around will require attention to core issues, such as supplying the basic human need for love and approval from legitimate sources, providing safe, nurturing living environments, and attaching value to each young man's existence.

I am certain that every young man grieving the death of his friend would jump at the chance to raise his buddy from the dead. Well, because of sin in the world, our sons will never totally eradicate death. However, they can raise their friends from the dead if they start while their friends are alive. The way our boys can be like Christ in raising people from the dead is by witnessing to them. Those friends will experience new life in Christ, and even if their physical lives are ended prematurely, they will live forever in heaven and have a fabulous reunion with our sons one day. Jesus said in John 5:24, "I tell you the truth, whoever hears my word and believes him who sent me has eternal life and will not be condemned; he has crossed over from death to life." And James 5:20 tells us, "Remember this: Whoever turns a sinner from

Step Aside
The National Association of School Psychologists published a paper titled *Helping Children Cope with Loss, Death, and Grief.* This user-friendly, four-page publication gives expert advice and can be found at www.nasponline.org. Once on the website, type into the search box "Helping children cope with loss."[1]

the error of his way will save him from death and cover over a multitude of sins."

Young people are about being "cool," "down," "fly," "the bomb," or whatever slang term is being used to define acceptance by the time you are reading this book. I have discovered that it is the confident kid who is actually the coolest kid. Therefore, work with your son to build his confidence and pride about being a child of God. Once he is secure in who he is as a Christian, no amount of teasing or put-downs can shake what he knows about himself. That kind of confidence rubs off, and he will soon find it effortless to share his faith with his friends. Talking about the Lord will be as simple as talking about basketball, cars, or even girls. The lifestyle of a happy, well-adjusted young man is a magnet for other young men.

I must mention here a young man I have used before as an example: Tyrod Anderson. I spoke of T.J. in chapter 6 as exemplary of a young man of integrity. What I didn't mention then is that this popular, good-looking, athletic student body leader and class valedictorian is also a strong Christian. He will not hesitate to reveal the fact that he loves God and desires to serve him. No one considers him a nerd for enthusiastically participating in chapel services and religion class discussions,

Step Aside

Is your son, one of his friends, or a boy in your community or church entangled in the self-destructive lifestyle of gang involvement, sexual promiscuity, or drug abuse? If so, perhaps you can begin the rescue process by answering and then acting upon even one of the following questions.

■ How can I (my church or a community program) supply this boy with the basic human need for love and approval?
■ Can I (my church or a community program) provide a safe, nurturing living environment for this young man?
■ How can I (my church or my community) communicate the value of this young man's existence?

and even if they did, that wouldn't bother him. He can converse as easily about faith as he can about football. His confidence in who he is in Christ contributes to his magnetism, and his friends respect him for it.

On the other hand, kids in school can be cruel sometimes; and let's face it—your son's admission that he is a Christian may bring him some flack. When Matthew was in fourth grade and I had to move him temporarily from private to public school, he experienced this firsthand. He had always carried his Bible to school, and he did so the first day of public school. Somehow the other kids in his class found out about it, took the Bible, and kicked it all around the playground during recess, commenting negatively about Christians and Christianity. The teacher didn't do very much about it either. This obviously was not the welcome we had anticipated; nevertheless, the incident didn't shake Matthew's confidence. In fact, he chalked it up to the fact that neither his classmates nor his teacher knew God, and that caused them to act as they did. He promptly, yet calmly, let them know that they would end up in hell if they did not have Christ in their lives.

Of course, that's when I got a call from the teacher.

It seems it was okay for the other kids to kick Matthew's Bible around and verbally disrespect his faith, but it wasn't okay for Matthew to take a stand and respond by expressing his evaluation of what they had done. I told her I was sorry her feelings were hurt by what Matthew had said, but I defended his right to have said it, especially in light of the fact that she had not reprimanded the other children for their wrong behavior. They had stolen Matthew's personal belongings, defaced his property, and mocked his religious beliefs. All of this violated Matthew's right to freedom of speech and freedom of religion, and it certainly smacked of blatant intolerance. I'm sure these actions would not have been allowed had the student been a Muslim, a Jew, or a member of any other religion. We came to an understanding that she would keep better tabs on her students' behavior regarding the rights of other children, while Matthew would stop telling kids they were going to hell. At home, Matthew and I discussed the meaning of the idiom "You can catch more flies with honey than with vinegar." I told him that witnessing after he had befriended people would probably be more effective than warnings about hell. A few weeks later, he quietly led one of his new friends to Christ.

Just how do you go about building Christian confidence into your son? The first and most vital step is to be sure to introduce your son to Jesus. Be sure he has a personal relationship with Christ, not just an acknowledgment of Christ's existence. Your son must be as sure of Christ in his life as he is of his own name.

Second, let your son know that he determines his own popularity. I polled fifty teenagers between the ages of fourteen and

Step Aside

Start a Christian confidence-building conversation. Ask your son, "What are you certain of? What can you do well without even really thinking about it?" Perhaps he is good at sports, Nintendo or PS2 game playing, math, making people laugh, taking things apart and putting them back together, tying his shoelaces, or something else. Let him know that he can be as confident that Christ is real and has his back as he is of whatever skill he possesses.

Build upon this confidence regularly. Make it a little game to see how many God-conversations you can have with others in a week. Maybe you can tell a coworker about an answered prayer and your son can invite a classmate to church. Maybe you can promise to pray for your boss's sick child and your son can refuse to lie and tell his friend he won't lie because he wants to obey the Ten Commandments. Maybe both of you can pray with friends to invite Christ into their hearts. Although no one really loses, at the end of the week, the one who has the most God-conversations gets treated to an ice cream cone.

seventeen and asked them, "What are the top three qualities you admire in people your age?" The answers surprised me. The top quality they admired was reliability, the fact that they could count on a person. Second was a sense of humor, and tied for third were being respectful and having hope for the future. Close behind these were two more qualities tied for fourth place—a positive attitude and the ability to speak up for themselves with confidence. These six qualities are hardly the list you would expect when the good-looking, well-dressed athletes are usually the ones surrounded by a slew of hangers-on. Let your son know that qualities like the ones in the poll are in reality what draws and keeps good friends. Help him cultivate and be comfortable with qualities that really matter, and he will attract similar people to him. There is nothing wrong with having a group of friends; the concern is the influence for bad or good that that circle of friends has on one another.

Handling the Death of Character

Death of character has to do with an attack on one's moral fiber. Even Jesus' character was called into question, so he can identify with your son if this monster ever rears its ugly head. Matthew 13:54-58 records an unsavory scene when, by doubting the validity and integrity of Jesus' teaching and miracles, Jesus' identity, character, and essential goodness were challenged.

> Coming to his hometown, he began teaching the people in their synagogue, and they were amazed. "Where did this man get this wisdom and these miraculous powers?" they asked. "Isn't this the carpenter's son? Isn't his mother's name Mary, and aren't his brothers James, Joseph, Simon and Judas? Aren't all his sisters with us? Where then did this man get all these things?" And they took offense at him. . . .
>
> And he did not do many miracles there because of their lack of faith.

Notice that the people of Jesus' hometown took offense at him. In other words, his very presence was a stumbling block for them. Why? Was he doing bad, hurtful, or embarrassing things? No, Jesus was teaching with wisdom and performing miracles. He was simply being who he said he was. That was an offense, because for those people to accept his works as authentic, they had to accept him as authentically sent of God as well. They had to agree that Jesus was on a higher plane than they, and that was simply too much to ask of their pride. So in order not to lift him up, they couldn't just leave him alone; they had to pull him down.

My paraphrase would be, "We know this guy. He's just like us; in fact, he's from around here. We don't understand how he's doing all this stuff, so we won't accept what he's saying." Consequently, Jesus could do no miracles among them because they lacked faith.

The questions about Jesus' authenticity came from the religious leaders—from church folks—as well. The Pharisees took the skepticism of Jesus' old neighbors to the next level of character assassination. They suggested that his miraculous powers came not from God but from the devil (see Matthew 12:22-37). Jesus' response demonstrates that he understood what the Pharisees were trying to do—to undermine his character by casting doubt on his actions. After all, a tree is recognized by its fruit (v. 33), and if Jesus acted through the Spirit of God, then he was, in fact, who he said he was—and the kingdom of God had come among the people (v. 28).

If Jesus had to face such challenges to his character, then your son's Christian character will also be tested. And as with the people from Jesus' hometown, the testers are likely to be people close to him: school acquaintances, work associates, girlfriends, possibly even kids from the church youth group. His testimony will cause others around him to feel offended. He will do things they neglect to do, or he will refrain from things in which they participate, and the difference will be stark, offensive, and a stumbling block. Rather than lift him up or just leave him alone, they are likely to do what they can to pull him down. When the only reason your son has for refusing to participate in some activity is because of his Christian commitment, what will he do if he hears comments like these: "Come on, church boy. You must think you're better than everybody else." "What's the matter, holy roller? Are you scared?" "Aw, he's a little punk. That's why he won't come with us."

The pressure to confirm to lower standards than those of Christ builds to a fever pitch in the middle and high school years. Prepare your son for these onslaughts by role-playing possible scenarios. Ask some what-would-you-do-if questions. Press him to formulate actual responses. Scripture says no temptation is going to come his way that is uncommon, but God will provide a way to escape sin's clutches (see 1 Corinthians 10:13). As a parent, equip him with escape mechanisms he can use for when his character is called into question.

Handling the Death of Friendship

Unfortunately, sometimes your son's standing up for the sake of his character may cause him to lose friends. At other times, your son may lose a friend because of a move, a breakup, or a misunderstanding. Jesus even lost friends from time to time; the most devastating losses were the times his friends cut out on him right when he needed them.

Above I mentioned the Scripture passage that told of Jesus being shunned in his own hometown. Even worse, in his darkest hour, Jesus' closest friends fell asleep on him, and Peter, usually his staunchest supporter, denied that he even knew Christ. I'm sure that Jesus felt real, emotional hurt in these incidences. What did he do? In the case of the hometown folks, I picture him lowering and shaking his head as he summarizes the incident by saying, "Only in his hometown and in his own house is a prophet without honor" (Matthew 13:57). When the fellas fell asleep, I picture that same head shaking with a furrowed brow, as Jesus says, "Are you still sleeping and resting? Look, the hour is near, and the Son of Man is betrayed into the hands of sinners. Rise, let us go! Here comes my betrayer!" (Matthew 26:45-46). And since Jesus had foretold Peter's denial, he dealt with Peter after the resurrection by verifying Peter's love for him, forgiving him, and reissuing the call to follow (see John 21). In these three responses lie some guidelines for helping our sons through the loss of friendships.

First, Jesus expressed the realization that sometimes those who are closest may give you the least support. Teach your son that not everybody is going to like him. He could lose a friend over something silly.

One of my students went through a problem with his best friend several years ago. The friend stopped talking to him. More than that, this friend started spreading rumors about him, attaching my student's name to some scandalous situations. It later came to light that the persecution had begun when my student started dating a particular girl—whom the friend also liked. When my student approached his friend to

Step Aside

Start your what-if questions with scenarios you formulate to match each character challenge related to obedience of the Ten Commandments. For example:

Commandment One: "You shall have no other gods before me" (Exodus 20:3). What if your baseball practice is scheduled for Sunday morning at 10:30 a.m., the same time we are supposed to be in church?

Commandment Two: "You shall not make for yourself an idol in the form of anything in heaven above or on the earth beneath or in the waters below" (Exodus 20:4). What if your coach gave you a rabbit's foot to rub on to give you luck before each game?

Commandment Five: "Honor your father and your mother" (Exodus 20:12). What if your friend tells you not to tell your parents that you took a detour on your way home from school to play video games at his uncle's house?

discuss things civilly, the guy refused to change his behavior, so the friendship was lost.

Most probably, not everyone will like your son. Moreover, not everyone will be impressed with him. He is going to have to be selective of those with whom he shares his dreams. When other people don't understand his dreams, they are likely to mock them in an effort to discourage him from even trying to fulfill them. This is called crab mentality: if you can't win, then no one can win.

> Crab mentality describes a way of thinking best described by the phrase "if I can't have it, neither can you." It is often used colloquially in reference to individuals or communities attempting to "escape" a so-called "underprivileged life," but kept from doing so by those others . . . attempting to ride upon their coat-tails or who simply resent their success. . . . In Hawaii it is known as the "alamihi syndrome," [meaning that these people] always manage to pull down the ones who are trying to climb up and over the sides of a bucket.[1]

Second, just as Jesus' buddies couldn't stay awake while he labored in prayer with God, your son must come to understand that his friends are not called to his calling. It is not his friends' responsibility to travel the roads God has directed him to travel, so he must not get discouraged when his friends don't value what he knows he has to do. In fact, he can—and probably should—lose friends who are not headed in the same direction he is going.

I have known Aaron Rousseau since he was in middle school. He never seems to fret over his individuality. Now a high school sophomore, he has been on high honor roll throughout all his years of school. When I asked him if he ever catches flack for doing something he is supposed to do, he answered with no hesitation, "Oh yes. I hear stuff about the abstinence thing all the time. Guys ask me if I'm going to 'do it,' and I tell them, 'No, I don't mess around.' They think that's pretty funny. Kids even tell me not to turn in my homework so they won't look bad. I just ignore them because I know what I'm doing is right and it's all going to pay off in the end."

Third, Jesus' outreach to forgive and restore Peter after the denial shows our boys the importance and power of forgiveness. Jesus' forgiving spirit provided the bridge Peter could use to cross back into a close relationship with his friend. Later Peter turned out to be the leader of the Jerusalem church.

Good friends are valuable. Even if your son's friends really disappoint him, he should know that the friendship might be restored through forgiveness on his part and humility on his friend's part. He will probably have to reach out to his friend first. He doesn't have to grovel; he just has to do or say something

Step Aside

Evaluate your son's ability to handle losing a friendship. If he hasn't faced this problem yet, now is a good time to equip him with the tools and understanding he will need to get through it when it happens. If he has gone through this or is presently going through it, these discussion starters may open the necessary conversation that will hopefully lead toward healing.

■ What are your thoughts when you discover someone you like does not like you?
■ Who is the leader among your group of friends? Why do the others listen to that person? What could that person request of you that you would not do? Exactly how would you refuse?
■ Are you being teased in school about anything?
■ Has anyone ever suggested that you disregard what you know is right? How did you react when this happened?
■ If you have ever been talked about before, how did you react?
■ Are there any friends in your life you need to forgive for doing you wrong?

small that would indicate an openness to talk once again. Guys can handle this very easily by starting up a basketball game or by riding skateboards down at the park at the same time. His gesture would build a bridge, letting the friend know it's safe to cross back over into friendship.

Handling the Death of Dreams

Sometimes the "friends" that die are our boys' dreams. No matter how much they may desire to make the team, get the girl, or land the job, it just might not happen. Jesus had high hopes for the people to whom he ministered, but after he did many miracles in certain cities and he saw that the people didn't repent, all he could do was lament over them (see Matthew 11:20-24).

There is nothing wrong with having high hopes, but your son can help himself to avoid unnecessary disappointment by setting attainable and probable goals. Face it: no child is good at everything, nor is he suited for everything. A kid who is great with words but bad with numbers need not set his sights on being an accountant or financial analyst. A boy who can spend hours in a lab or garage working with his hands to produce a product won't feel total fulfillment as part of a think tank.

Assist your son in tailoring his dreams to turn them into attainable and realistic goals. Notice I said "goals," plural. There's wisdom in the adage "Don't put all your eggs in one basket." Set the goals far enough out of immediate reach to necessitate effort, but not so far out as to invite disillusionment. Direct your son toward attainment and keep in sight the fact that the pain of missing one goal is soothed when he has plans B and C in the wings.

NOTE
1. "Crab Mentality," http://en.wikipedia.org/wiki/Crab_mentality.

12
The Savior Crucified

Even though I knew the ending to the heart-wrenching Mel Gibson movie *The Passion of the Christ*, the crucifixion was still disturbing to watch. I kept thinking, *He's doing this for me; he's doing this for me.* Jesus' death was all about fulfilling the purpose of God to atone for the sins of the world. But if there had been a plan B available to bypass the painful and gruesome ordeal of the cross, Jesus would have taken it. He agonized about this with God three times (see Matthew 26:39-44). In the end Jesus submitted to God's plan. The most poignant lesson our sons can learn here from Jesus' example is that he disregarded what he wanted in favor of the cause of God. Being like Jesus, then, means dying to self for God's purposes. As we explore how Christ dealt with his arrest, trials, and crucifixion, we will see the importance of developing the Christlike characteristics of *accepting God's purpose as fate, handling enemies properly,* and *suffering without complaint.*

Accepting God's Purpose as Fate

In Matthew 26 and Mark 14, Jesus is in the Garden of Gethsemane praying because he knows he is facing death. In many other passages, we see his divinity: he heals the sick, gives sight to the blind, forgives sin, and raises the dead; but in these two passages, we clearly see his humanity. How reflective of us is his thrice-made plea to avoid the cross (see especially Matthew 26:36-44). As God, Jesus knew what was coming and realized that the fragile human body he was wearing during his earth visit would be horrendously broken under the agony. Much more than the expectation of the bodily pain, however, was the anticipation of the agony of having to take on the sins of the world. If I had been allowed the foreknowledge of even half the painful situations I have faced in life, I would have done my best to opt out too. So would you. Yet Jesus overcame the yearnings of his flesh for release from his fate. How did he do it? He rejected his wants by accepting God's will. He declined his desire by complying with God's design. He abandoned his rights by submitting to God's requirement.

Our sons will learn to accept God's purpose for their lives only if they are willing to give up their own. Getting to this place takes trust in God. How do we teach our sons to trust God? They learn to trust God, the ultimate authority figure, if they can trust us—their parents—the authority figures God has ordained for them here on earth. I also believe it to be God's perfect plan for boys to receive that picture of trusting him as their Father through experiencing a relationship of trust with their earthly fathers.

My friend Al Starr, pastor of Ascension Lutheran Church in Los Angeles, California, related a story about his son that makes this point perfectly.

> One night, when Temesghen was about four years old, I heard his congested cough at midnight, and it was my turn to get up. The telltale wheezing sent me straight to the medicine cabinet for his asthma prescription; the granules were to be mixed into a spoonful of applesauce.
>
> When I returned from the kitchen to the bathroom, my little guy was standing on the rug right in front of the toilet, every breath a struggle. I said to him, "Here, this will help you breathe better." I sat down in front of him and extended the spoonful of applesauce and medicine.

It wasn't what he said and not even how he said it but what came with his response that startled me. "No" was the only word, but the accompanying look and attitude relayed the message, "And you can't make me." It was no surprise to me that he didn't want the medicine because the applesauce did little to disguise the awful taste, but here I was, face-to-face not just with resistance, but with a spirit of defiance. As sick as he was, as little as he was, he was taking a stand.

In the next few moments of looking into my son's face, my mind fast forwarded and I saw myself looking into his face and that spirit at age twelve. The spirit of defiance was threatening to divide us. I said to him, "Little brother, I admire your determination, but I can't let you win this one. You can't step one foot off that rug until you take your medicine." He said nothing, and I walked out of the bathroom.

I went back to check on him in a couple of minutes and every few minutes for the next hour and a half. "Ready for your medicine?" I would ask. "No," would come his wheezed response. His weak eyes and heaving chest let me know that the asthma was causing him great discomfort but somehow not enough to prevent him from putting us through this fight to have things his own way. Finally, after four and a half hours, he looked at me with tears in his eyes and said, "Help me, Daddy."

Pastor Starr proved that Temesghen could trust him by continually being there to offer the only relief available. Temesghen didn't receive the medicine until he bent his will to accept it. The nasty taste didn't change, and he added hours to his suffering by his stubborn refusal to yield. In the end, he did what his daddy said he had to do.

Likewise, our sons must be taught to bend their wills to receive what God has to offer. Then and only then will they receive what they need, and then trust will be built. Too often we confuse need with greed and tend to associate trusting God with having him fulfill all our lusts. So wrong. Trusting God has to do with the knowledge that he is who he says he is, and he is sovereign. We live to fulfill his purpose, not the other way around. His word is the last word, and we have no other choice but to live by what God has said.

How do we communicate this principle? Perhaps our boys ought not to receive some blessings from our hands until their wills are brought into line with God's Word. Children who can't pleasantly obey authority should not be rewarded. If Johnny can't obey his teacher, Johnny can't ride his bike. The pay normally given for chores should be withheld if they are done incompletely and incorrectly. Do you feel you should pay the construction worker on your house for shoddy workmanship? And stick to punishments assigned to unruly or inappropriate behavior.

Perhaps the "affluenza" with which our boys suffer is directly linked to our injection of too much unearned "stuff" into their lives. The longer this disease is allowed to spread, the more deeply rooted is the sense of entitlement. Kids translate your generosity into debt, feeling you owe them the extras. Why should they trust their heavenly Parent to supply their needs when they can turn to their earthly parents and get "greeds" fulfilled with little to no effort at all? If they do receive special wants, make sure they have put forth very special effort. This will lead to an increased sense of appreciation, gratefulness, and responsibility once the request is granted.

When our son Jerod was in high school, he was messing

Step Aside

- List your son's needs and "greeds."
- Does he receive any "greeds" he has done nothing to earn?
- Evaluate the requirements you place on your son for earning his special wants. Are the requirements fair? Are they too lax so they require no significant effort? Are they too strict so as to be unattainable?

around and not concentrating on his school work; consequently, he was bringing home poor grades. He wanted a car, but with those grades, he could forget it. His dad decided to set the bar very high in order to encourage him to pull up his grades. Figuring his checkbook was safe; his dad told him he would buy him a car if he got straight A's. Jerod embarked on a mission. Wouldn't you know that kid came home with straight A's on his next report card? His dad could be trusted, so Jerod was on wheels soon after.

We can teach our boys to trust God by mirroring God's care for them through us. Supply them with their needs. Attach the attainment of extras to appropriate behavior and to being earned. Set reasonable goals that are challenging yet achievable.

As our boys grow older, they will get to the place where they will need to ask God for help we can't supply. They will also reach crossroads where either their wants or God's will must be chosen before they can move on. If they have watched us trust God and we have built a legacy of trust into them by not having jumped to their every whim, when they reach these junctures, they will readily know that it is right to surrender their wills and trust God for themselves. They will know that the longer they live in defiance of God, the longer they will suffer and the worse the suffering will get. They will know as Jesus knew that God's will is their fate, and it is best for them and everyone around them if they simply submit to it.

Handling Enemies Properly

An enemy can be handled in several ways. Sometimes fear dictates how we handle an enemy. In the Los Angeles area where I live, we have learned that road rage is real. We think twice about screaming our disapproval at an erratic driver because we don't want to end up the victim of a freeway shooting. Airports all around the world have transformed their lobbies into high-tech security centers thanks to enemies seeking to terrorize the planet into submission. Fear makes us avoid enemies, caution makes us handle them from a distance, and courage prompts ordinary people to act heroically, facing down an enemy who is attacking a defenseless person.

Fear, caution, and courage are indeed ways to deal with enemies, but Jesus shows us two efficient and effective methods that put enemies in their place. He faced down his enemies by continuing to do the right thing himself, confronting them face-to-face with the truth, but he also understood their shortcomings.

Jesus collected enemies simply by doing the right thing. During his entire ministry, he butted heads with those who constantly challenged his message and his identity. In the end, false accusations got him arrested and crucified. Through it all, Jesus faced down his enemies by continuing to teach, heal, love, and make a difference by always doing the exact right thing.

My friend Linda shared with me a conversation she and her nine-year-old son, Sammie, had about a tough situation he faced at school. Their conversation started with Sammie's question, "Mom, can we talk?"

Linda could tell by his face that something serious had happened, so in the most controlled tone she could muster over the butterflies beginning to awaken, she said, "Sure son, what's up?"

Sammie then proceeded to paint a blow-by-blow picture of other boys at school singing and dancing to vulgar music. When he did not have a clue which group they were copying, he was mocked and derided for being totally out of it.

Linda asked Sammie what happened next, and he explained, "I told them it wasn't something my parents would approve of and I didn't like the words anyway. Then I walked away."

Immediately her heart sank. "I'm sorry, sweetheart," she responded. "You'll make more friends."

"What are you talking about, Mom?" Sammie stared at her with a puzzled look. "We're still friends. After I walked away, they found me and we went back to doing our regular stuff."

"Then everything is okay? Why did you bring it up?" she asked.

"I told you because I knew you would want to know. Sometimes you have to do the right thing even when the other guys don't."

Sammie had enough intestinal fortitude to stand for what was right even though his buddies were doing wrong.

You can tell by the conversation between Sammie and his mom that they had a close relationship. We build the strength to stand into our sons by fostering an atmosphere of openness no matter what. The confidence gained by being able to be honest with us about anything will enable them to be honest with enemies or friends about what's right and will ultimately engender an honesty with God.

Adam admired his dad and carried a deep desire to please him. The great grades, the wise judgments, even the choices in friends, were all proud accomplishments that brought Adam his father's praise. So when Adam made a bonehead decision in his late teens, he experienced an overwhelming amount of anxiety about facing his father. He avoided the very person who could be the most helpful because he feared that his failure would erase his father's love.

Step Aside

■ Does your son feel comfortable coming to you to discuss absolutely anything, or is he so fearful of your disapproval that he doesn't give you a chance to hear what he is going through?

■ How can you support your son yet not approve of his wrong or bad decision?

■ Does your son honor truth? How do you know?

■ Help your son identify the weapons that are fashioned to hurt him and then pray Isaiah 54:17 over each one discovered. Weapons can be tangible, wielded from without, and easily identifiable, such as Johnny the bully or a coach who has it out for him. Or they can be spiritual, subtle, and much harder to defeat, such as the spirit of defiance, greed, jealousy, inordinate anger, pride, etc.

Please don't allow that to be the case with your son. Love must remain unconditional. Neither smarts nor boneheadedness can be allowed to be the basis of your relationship. You don't become God's enemy when you make a stupid decision, so your son should not feel alienated because he makes a poor choice. The only way your son will know your relationship is based on love, not performance, is if you relate to him in the same way whether he's up or down.

Does that mean you accept the wrong he does? No, not at all. But if you talk to him when he has done well, you should still talk to him when he has done poorly. Sure the conversation is different, but communication remains in order. If you are there for him, basking with him in the glow of his achievements when he is receiving acclaim; you need to be there for him, walking with him through the darkness when he is at his worse.

When Walter Lee Younger loses all the insurance money and crushes the family's dreams in the critically acclaimed stage play *A Raisin in the Sun* by Lorraine Hansberry, Mama chides his sister Beneatha for despising him. She says, "Child, when do you think is the time to love somebody the most; when they done good and made things easy for everybody? Well then, you ain't through learning—because that ain't the time at all. It's when he's at his lowest and can't believe in hisself 'cause the world done whipped him so. When you starts measuring somebody, measure him right child, measure him right."[1]

Not only did Jesus always stand for what was right, but he also never seemed to tire of confronting his enemies face-to-face with the truth. Calling the religious leaders a "generation of vipers" was not exactly a great way to win friends and influence people, but he did it because that was a true assessment of their inner identity (see Matthew 23:33 KJV). He reasoned with people with honest questions, cut to the core of the issue when people's intentions were less than upright, and physically drove money changers out of his Father's temple. He was not hesitant to say things people wouldn't understand.

To be like Christ, our sons must trust truth. We teach them to trust the truth by honoring it ourselves, rewarding it when appropriate, dispensing it when necessary, and always allowing it to have its way. The truth will always win out in the end; there is no need for endless self-justification. In John 8:31-32 we find Jesus saying, "If you hold to my teaching, you are really my disciples. Then you will know the truth, and the truth will set you free."

Finally, concerning dealing with enemies, Jesus understood his enemies' shortcomings. While dying on the cross, Jesus made a request in favor of his enemies. "Father, forgive them, for they do not know what they are doing" (Luke 23:34). Jesus didn't worry about his enemies; he turned them over to God for him to deal with them.

This is a tough principle to teach our boys. By nature, boys want to right wrongs and set people straight. But being like Jesus in regard to enemies means our boys must exercise trust in God to take care of their enemies. The Bible instructs us to behave totally opposite from our feelings when it comes to contentious people. Romans 12:19-21 instructs, "Do not take revenge, my friends, but leave room for God's wrath, for it is written: 'It is mine to avenge; I will repay,' says the Lord. On the contrary: 'If your enemy is hungry, feed him; if he is thirsty, give him something to drink. In doing this, you will heap burning coals on his head.' Do not be overcome by evil, but overcome evil with good."

You may be thinking, "Doesn't the point you just made about facing enemies head-on contradict with turning them over to God?" No. These two seeming extremes should actually happen simultaneously. Our boys need to face adversaries head-on while turning them over to God. God will give our boys the words and actions necessary to handle enemies on a case-by-case basis. Being the butt of jokes or the one everyone picks on is no fun at all, but God knows the soft underbelly of the meanie, the bully, and the instigator. He even knows how to battle unseen enemies.

When Alexander was thirteen-years-old, someone put a MySpace page together on him that posted his picture, his full name, and the statement "I am a homosexual." It went on to proclaim what he supposedly liked to do to men.

The page was discovered by Alexander's cousin in another state. She had her mother call Alex's parents immediately. When his parents sat down with him, he felt humiliated. The profile had been set up a year before. Although Alex said he had never been harassed in school about it, he didn't want to go to school until the page was off the Web. They prayed together, asking God for guidance. His parents told him that Satan uses what works against us, and if Alex folded and hid, Satan would have ammunition against him the rest of his life. They counseled him to stand strong, go to school, and face whatever God allowed to come his way.

Alexander agreed, and the next morning, the family gathered for special prayer before he went to school. That day they contacted MySpace, and by noon the site had been removed. His mom tried to call Alex at school, but she discovered later that his cell phone had been stolen at lunch. He quickly added, "Satan couldn't get me with MySpace, so he tried to trip me up by having my phone taken. No problem. God is my strength. I can handle it."

God and his Word are real and powerful. Encourage your son with the fact that although Satan will throw every possible distraction his way, God promises in Scripture that, "'no weapon forged against you will prevail, and you will refute every tongue that accuses you. This is the heritage of the servants of the LORD, and this is their vindication from me,' declares the LORD" (Isaiah 54:17).

Suffering without Complaint

The third characteristic to build within our sons that we will here glean from Jesus' final ordeal is the manner in which he suffered without complaint. Simply said, Jesus did what he had to do even though it was hard. He suffered through the indignities even though he had the power to stop everything that was going on. He allowed the unfair treatment to continue even knowing he was actually being good to the people who were causing him the pain. He hung and died on a cross that had been hewn from a tree he created.

Maturity is not measured in reaching a level at which one can do whatever he chooses. Maturity is measured by reaching a level at which one chooses to do what he must. Why don't young men see the need to defend their country? Why do young men want to move straight from C-level high school work to a management position in the business world? Why do young men make babies but refuse to raise the children? Why is it that so many of our young men want something for nothing? Consider this scenario: Members of the builder generation erected churches, colleges, and business institutions by the sweat of their brow and even, during the Civil Rights Movement, by the shedding of their blood. They produced the baby boomers who have grown up in relative privilege, with education and opportunity available and within reach. The boomers raised the busters who, now two generations away from the struggles that earned them their ease, are largely oblivious to the price it cost their ancestors to achieve such success. In each successive generation, a sense of entitlement to prosperity and ease only seems to grow.

We are responsible for teaching our boys that being like Jesus means following his example of suffering—doing what must be done—without complaint. A contemporary application of this principle would involve work and responsibility. Work need not be drudgery. In fact, the first man, Adam, was given a job as soon as he was created. Genesis 2:15 says, "The LORD God took the man and put him in the Garden of Eden to work it and take care of it." Work became a form of suffering when Adam sold us over to the sin nature.

The ability to rejoice in honorable work is a way to exemplify the reality of Christ in one's life. It is imperative that we teach our boys to have pride in themselves for a job well done, for responsibilities borne, rather than for how much work they were able to avoid. It was a sad commentary when several young men on a recent field

Step Aside

Read over the following Scriptures with your son. Discuss God's view of work and pray with him that his heart catches God's vision of work.

■ "Those who sow in tears will reap with songs of joy. He who goes out weeping, carrying seed to sow, will return with songs of joy, carrying sheaves with him" (Psalm 126:5-6).

■ "The wicked man earns deceptive wages, but he who sows righteousness reaps a sure reward" (Proverbs 11:18).

■ "One who is slack in his work is brother to one who destroys" (Proverbs 18:9).

■ "Finish your outdoor work and get your fields ready; after that, build your house" (Proverbs 24:27).

■ "But a married man is concerned about the affairs of this world—how he can please his wife" (1 Corinthians 7:33).

■ "The one who sows to please his sinful nature, from that nature will reap destruction; the one who sows to please the Spirit, from the Spirit will reap eternal life. Let us not become weary in doing good, for at the proper time we will reap a harvest if we do not give up" (Galatians 6:8-9).

■ "He who has been stealing must steal no longer, but must work, doing something useful with his own hands, that he may have something to share with those in need" (Ephesians 4:28).

■ "Make it your ambition to lead a quiet life, to mind your own business and to work with your hands" (1 Thessalonians 4:11).

■ "For even when we were with you, we gave you this rule: 'If a man will not work, he shall not eat'" (2 Thessalonians 3:10).

■ "If anyone does not provide for his relatives, and especially for his immediate family, he has denied the faith and is worse than an unbeliever" (1 Timothy 5:8).

■ "Our people must learn to devote themselves to doing what is good, in order that they may provide for daily necessities and not live unproductive lives" (Titus 3:14).

trip thought they had "gotten over" when one of the teachers paid their lunch restaurant tab because they didn't have enough to cover it. Instead of feeling embarrassed and immediately making plans to repay the teacher, the boys bragged about getting away without paying for their food.

It is natural for a young man to want to work; it is unnatural for him to want to waste his life away. Believe it or not, the gang culture proves this. According to the 2004 National Youth Gang Survey, "approximately 760,000 gang members and 24,000 gangs were active in more than 2,900 jurisdictions that city (population of 2,500 or more) and county law enforcement agencies served in 2004."[2] It takes a tremendous amount of work and organizational skill to run an association consisting of hundreds of thousands of members. These young men crave involvement and worth. Just think of the corporate giants these guys could be if their eyes could be focused on using their energies for productive causes.

As parents, we must start by shifting our values if we ever expect our sons to see any benefit in good old-fashioned hard work. Nothing of any lasting value is obtained easily. Our personal estimate of success cannot be centered on how much money is made, but on the quality of life brought about by involvement in work that matters. We can only extinguish the shine of the dollar signs in our boys' eyes by focusing the spotlight on the message of quality, responsibility, and honor. Our boys must be exposed to successful, honest men more than they are to rich, dishonest ones.

We preach, "Get an education. Get a job. Be active in your church. Take care of your family." But do our sons then see us esteeming those activities or hear us spewing comments such as, "College is too expensive"; "I can't wait to leave my job"; "They ask me to spend too much time down at that church"; "She got pregnant on purpose just to trap him"?

By his later teens, your son's heart should be sold on the principle of work. His purpose on the planet is to serve God, and he will do that best in the capacity for which God has suited him. Whatever form it might take, service, by definition, is work.

Your son will be like Jesus when he dies to himself by accepting God's purpose as his fate, handling enemies properly, and suffering without complaint. The development of these characteristics will issue forth from a humble heart. Christ's crucifixion defines humility: power under control.

But this is not the end of the story. Just as Jesus Christ would have been no use to us as a dead Savior, our sons are no use to the world as reclusive ascetics, staying quiet behind the scenes, trying hard not to make waves. No. Our sons must proclaim with Paul the words of Galatians 2:20, "I am crucified with Christ: nevertheless I live; yet not I, but Christ liveth in me: and the life which I now live in the flesh I live by the faith of the Son of God, who loved me, and gave himself for me" (KJV). Let's usher our sons through the experience of death to their sins and into the experience of living an abundant life in Christ.

NOTES

1. Lorraine Hansberry, *A Raisin in the Sun*, act 3.
2. Arlen Egley Jr. and Christina E. Ritz, Highlights of the 2004 National Youth Gang Survey, U.S. Department of Justice Fact Sheet, April 2006, #1 http://www.ncjrs.gov/pdffiles1.

13
The Resurrected Lord

In Romans 6 Paul gives us an amazingly precise explanation of how we Christians, including our believing sons, relate to Jesus through his death and resurrection. Since I can't explain the relationship any better than Paul, through the inspiration of God's Spirit, has already done, let's read that explanation here:

> We were therefore buried with him through baptism into death in order that, just as Christ was raised from the dead through the glory of the Father, we too may live a new life. If we have been united with him like this in his death, we will certainly also be united with him in his resurrection. For we know that our old self was crucified with him so that the body of sin might be done away with, that we should no longer be slaves to sin—because anyone who has died has been freed from sin. Now if we died with Christ, we believe that we will also live with him. (Romans 6:4-8)

In short, our boys who have identified with Christ in his death have appropriated his work on the cross by dying to their own sins. They can now reflect the image of Christ because they can operate in the world focused on God's purpose for their lives. So as our sons live for Christ, let's look at the resurrection, focusing on three actions of the Savior from which we can extract principles to help our sons continue to reflect Christ's image. When we observe our risen Lord, we see that he raised himself, he revealed himself, and he represents us before God.

Jesus Raised Himself

Since Jesus is God, he indeed did raise himself from the dead. He said he would before he died. "Destroy this temple, and I will raise it again in three days," he said. "But the temple he had spoken of was his body" (John 2:19, 21). Never again would he be the Suffering Servant. Never again would men lift their hands to arrest, beat, slap, whip, or nail him. From now on, men's hands would either be lifted in praise to him or stretched out in pity for themselves at having missed him along life's way.

You may not believe in the authenticity of the Shroud of Turin, but something about its claims makes an extremely important theological point. The image of the crucified man on the shroud is like the negative of a photograph. A negative image is produced by a sudden, very bright flash of light burning onto an object, in this case, onto the cloth. The image on the shroud is burned in such a way that the light had to come from within the cloth, not outside of it. In other words, when we are looking at the negative image burned onto the Shroud of Turin, we could literally be seeing the very moment of the resurrection. This would prove Christ's claim of his ability to raise himself. Light came from within Christ, and life burned the proof right onto that flimsy wrap. In hindsight it is easy now to question how anyone could have thought an earthen tomb and some wrapped pieces of fabric could hold the Author of life. God is in control.

Don't be surprised when your son wants to rise up and take control. Every boy wants that; it's inbred, because humans are made in the image of God. Your son was born with the desire to be in control of what God gives him to manage. Unfortunately, the sin nature, with which he was also born, has tarnished the image of God within, so now, even though your son is supposed to make Spirit-directed decisions, many times he forges ahead stubbornly, seeking to control in unwise ways. As a baby, he says, "I can do it." As an elementary kid, he's a daredevil on his bike or skateboard, attempting to control gravity if it were possible. In middle school his style of dress changes to say, "I am in control of my own identity." In high school he drives too fast, listens to music that's too loud, hangs out with girls who are too racy, stays up too late, and challenges every rule of the house and organized institutions, all in an effort to test the limits of control. This challenging continues into young adulthood when he indiscriminately changes his major, longs to explore the world, and opens credit card accounts he doesn't need. It's all about control.

It's the parents' job, not to destroy, but to fine-tune that control gene.

Ruth's son Gabriel once decided he wanted to secede from the family. "It's your choice," Ruth told him. "However, be aware that if you take yourself out from under our parental authority, you will then be directly under God's authority and directly accountable to him." She went on to remind him that God knows his every action, word, and thought. Gabriel reconsidered. The issue never came up again, and his attitude went through a significant transformation.

The boy reflecting the image of Christ may make some pretty silly choices, but even if the mistakes cost him embarrassment, debt, or injury, he can learn from them. Nurture the fact that wanting to be in

> **Step Aside**
> No matter his age, observe your son's efforts at control. Be careful to separate acts of mature independence from acts of defiance. Give direction regarding the proper attitude he should exhibit. A godly leader controls with confidence, not with intimidation.

control is a godly characteristic of manhood, but wisdom about what to control and how to control it completes the picture. Like Jesus did, your son must learn to rise up when he is knocked down and take responsibility for what he must do.

Jesus Revealed Himself

Luke 24 records the events on the morning of the resurrection. Jesus started showing up, just popping in to greet his friends—friends who saw him die three days earlier. The following is an excerpt from verses 13-39:

> Now that same day two of them were going to a village called Emmaus. . . . As they talked and discussed these things with each other, Jesus himself came up and walked along with them. . . . And beginning with Moses and all the Prophets, he explained to them what was said in all the Scriptures concerning himself. . . . Then their eyes were opened and they recognized him. . . . Look at my hands and my feet. It is I myself! Touch me and see."

Jesus knew it was important for him to reveal himself clearly in order for his followers to relate to him correctly. Jesus revealed himself through his testimony and his touch. Not only did he proclaim who he was, but he allowed people to get close enough to him to touch him, to handle him and prove to themselves that he was real.

Our sons can emulate Christ in the same way. First, we can teach our boys to be proud of who they are as Christians and testify to it. Being a Christian doesn't make you a sissy or a little punk. Jesus spoke up without reservation, proclaiming the truth unashamedly. Jesus walked in confidence, knowing full well who he was and being proud of that. He was comfortable with the reality of his being.

This kind of comfort level starts in the home. We build this self-acceptance in our sons by balancing the out-of-control control gene we spoke about above with opportunities for them to be independent and responsible with healthy and honorable decisions. Small successes strengthen the foundation that girds up our sons' self-esteem.

We also need to teach our boys some basic apologetics, for they need to know how to answer challenges to their Christian beliefs. Armed with confidence, pride in their convictions, and answers for their critics, even when their Christian principles are challenged, they will have the strength to stand. They will be the ones who won't steal from the corner store, cheat on a test, plagiarize a term paper, experiment with drugs, or have premarital sex.

In addition to revealing himself through his testimony, your son can be like Christ by being real enough to touch. In other words, he should cultivate a friendly persona that says, like Jesus said, "It is I myself! Touch me and see." Okay, so he probably wouldn't use those exact words today, but others can't be affected by his life unless they are allowed to get close enough for them to see that he is real.

Kids have keen radar that can sense a phony a mile away, so they are already wired to detest being fake. But for all their efforts at nonconformity to what they consider "the system," kids still spend an enormous amount of energy, no doubt enticed by the culture, to conform to the latest fads and trends. If they don't wear the right brand of sneakers, T-shirts, and jeans, or carry the newest trend in cell phones, they feel extremely "uncool." Again, parents, it's our job to get involved. Point out the areas in which your son is just trying to go along with the crowd. Bring his attention to changes he makes to please others rather than for his own good or advancement.

Ruth mentored several young men from her church and community who became as close as her own son. When one of these heart-adopted sons made plans for a first date with a certain young woman, he thought smoking a little pot "would add a nice touch." Knowing how important it was to him for people to be themselves and not be phony, she asked, "How will you know who you really are if you alter yourselves with pot?" The logic worked. Ruth then suggested that if he wanted to take the girl a plant of some kind, flowers may seem corny, but girls still appreciate them. The girl got flowers.

Jesus Represents Us

Ever since his ascension, Jesus has been interceding for us. Jesus talks to God about us, which in turn empowers us. Think of it: Jesus talks to God about your son. Romans 8:34 says, "Christ Jesus, who died—more than that, who was raised to life—is at the right hand of God and is also interceding for us."

Notice here Jesus' location as he talks to God. Where is he? He is at the right hand of God. The right hand is the hand of power. In other words, Jesus has constant access to the power of God. He is talking to God about us to empower us.

If our sons are to be like Christ, they too must maintain their position through Jesus with direct access to the power of God. Impassioned by this power, their lives should be lived ever in search of ways to empower the lives of others. Encourage your son to go beyond just living his life as a testimony to Christ to work toward a career or vocation that will touch the lives of others in a positive way.

The story of Ty, my friend Linda Jewell's only son, is perfect not only to illustrate this point, but to end this book. Always the observant eagle-eye, when Ty was a teenager out on a leisurely fishing trip with his family, he pointed across the ruffled waters. "Over there! It looks like a woman with little kids in a motorboat. But she's rowing. Maybe she's in trouble."

They opened the throttle and sped toward the distant speck. As they approached, sure

> **Step Aside**
> Ask your son if his friends know that he is a Christian. If not, why not? If so, how do they know? Read and discuss the Robert Frost poem "The Road Not Taken."[1]

enough, a woman and her two young children began to wave frantically. They pulled alongside, and the desperate mother explained that the motor had died. With no drama or theatrics, Linda's father and Ty hooked a rope to the powerless boat and towed it with the woman and her children safely back to the marina.

The years passed. Ty became a commander of almost two hundred soldiers in a war zone, and the military entrusted him with specific missions. The teenager who saw a speck in the distance on a lake and did all he could to help became accustomed to rescuing others in distress and, as much as humanly possible, bringing them back safely.

Living as Christ lived is all about living a life of service—service to God and to others. Raising our sons to be like Christ boils all the pages of this book down into the Master's statement of the greatest commandment in Matthew 22:37-40. "'Love the Lord your God with all your heart and with all your soul and with all your mind.' This is the first and greatest commandment. And the second is like it: 'Love your neighbor as yourself.' All the Law and the Prophets hang on these two commandments."

We parents of boys have both a huge responsibility and tremendous privilege to partner with God in raising our sons to be like Christ. As we prayerfully, determinedly, and joyfully perform our duty in this profession, we will look up at our male offspring one day and thankfully proclaim, "Thank God, that's my son in his image."

NOTE

1. Robert Frost, "The Road Not Taken," *Mountain Interval*, 1920, http://www.bartleby.com.